Quick & Easy Pages

by Joanna Campbell Slan

columnist for

**Books by
Joanna Slan:**

**Scrapbook Story-
telling** (EFG)

**Scrapbook Story-
telling: Story-
telling with Rub-
ber Stamps** (EFG)

**Using Stories and
Humor: Grab Your
Audience**
(Allyn & Bacon)

**I'm Too Blessed to
Be Depressed**
(Wildhorse Creek
Press)

**Contributions by
Joanna Slan**

"Directory Assistance"
**4th Course of
Chicken Soup for
the Soul**

"Damaged Goods"
**Chicken Soup for
the Couple's Soul**

"Climbing the Stair-
way to Heaven"
**Chicken Soup for
the Soul at Work**

"The Scar"
**Chicken Soup for a
Woman's Soul,
Vol. II**

"And I Almost Didn't
Go", "The Last of the
Big, Big Spenders"
**Chocolate for a
Woman's Soul**

"United States of
Motherhood"
**Chocolate for a
Woman's Heart**

**Chicken Soup for
the Expectant
Mother's Soul**

Cover and inside pages:
Photography and design:
VIP Graphics
St. Louis, MO
(314) 535-1117

Hand sketch:
Bill Perry

Dedicated to my mother, Joanna F. Campbell
"Thanks for teaching me to use my noodle, Mom."

Acknowledgements. Thanks to the sales team at F&W Publications, especially Laura Smith for believing in the power of creating a series. Thanks
also to the incredible team at *Creating Keepsakes* Scrapbook Magazine for believing in what I have to say about saving stories and giving me a chance to
be a columnist. Many accolades to the manufacturers who sent supplies to
showcase. And special thanks to my friends who are parents of the "other"
children in my life. You honor me by letting me share in the joy of your
children.

Scrapbook Storytelling: Quick & Easy Pages

First Edition. Printed and bound in the United States of America.
04 03 02 01 00   5 4 3 2 1

Library of Congress Catalog Card Number 00-107522
ISBN: 1-930500-02-5

Trademarks and Copyrights. Scrapbook Storytelling is a trademark of
Paperdolls of St. Louis. Throughout this book, the author and publisher
have made every attempt to respect copyrighted and trademarked material. In the case of accidental infringement, please contact the publisher to
make corrections for future reprints and editions. For instances when the
trademark symbol has not been used, the author and publisher had no in-
tention of infringing upon that trademark. Manufacturers and suppliers
and their trademarks are listed on the Web site, www.scrapbookstory-
telling.com.

Publisher:
EFG, Inc.
savetales@aol.com
www.scrapbookstorytelling.com

Distributed to the trade by:
Betterway Books & North Light Books
Imprints of F&W Publications
1507 Dana Ave., Cincinnati, OH 45207
(800) 289-0963; fax: (513) 531-4082

Contents

NOTES:

Why the Journaling Boxes are Empty

After a quick glance, you'll see that the journaling boxes on the sample scrapbook pages of this book are empty.

(Don't despair—I still share the stories behind the pages and am also working on a companion book showing journaling techniques, *One Minute Journaling*.)

Here's why: Page creation is a right brain activity and journaling is a left brain activity. By splitting your efforts into two distinct activities, you'll avoid the stop/start hesitation that occurs as you try to move between two opposing activities.

As a result, you'll get more done, get more down, and get more pleasure from both laying out pages and writing.

Welcome to Quick & Easy Pages

One Christmas, Santa brought me a doll named Sharon. She came with a complete wardrobe that my mother had sat up nights sewing. Before long, my mother was teaching me to sew, too.

One of my mother's gifts is an ability to break down complex ideas. It wasn't until I took home economics that I learned the "real" way to put in a zipper and set in a sleeve. These methods were more fraught with problems than Mom's way. Because she was self-taught, Mom had found easier, quicker ways than those of the "experts."

This is the spirit of *Quick & Easy Pages*—information in a simple, streamlined, nearly goof-proof way. Once in a while, you'll want to spend time scrapbooking a complex page design. That's fine. But, complex isn't always the best choice when you have limited time, a huge pile of photos, and a family life providing both interruptions and stories to save. For those times, you can turn to this book for inspiration and direction.

How to Use this Book

To make this book useful, I've given you lots of options for diving in, picking up a pearl or two, and surfacing. You don't have to read from cover to cover to find value, although I hope that you eventually read it all so you don't miss a single good idea.

Time-consuming layouts do not necessarily produce better pages. Sometimes your story gets lost in a blitz of overproduction. On the other hand, quick and easy pages can be GREAT pages. The more you know about layout, the more you pare down and focus, the more you plan before you paste down, the faster your pages will go. Enjoy!

What Makes a Page Quick & Easy?

I've done pages in 15 minutes, and I've worked for 10 hours or more on pages. A page is quick and easy when you do the following:

1. Limit your cropping and matting—without losing your photos' impact.
2. Create appropriate headlines or page titles quickly.
3. Use time-saving techniques that speed your routine scrapbooking steps.
4. Make your tools work for you, using them easily with few mistakes.
5. Plan Sites of Future Journaling (SoFJ), which allow you to journal later.

TECHNIQUE: *Matting Journaling Boxes & Photos*

On the right-hand pages of this book you'll learn a scrapbooking technique. We start with matting, a technique that you'll use often.

◄ Attach your photo or journaling box to your matting paper with one square of double-sided tape.

Lift the arm and slide your paper ► onto the paper trimmer. Line up the bottom of the paper so that it is flush with the bottom of the paper trimmer.

◄ Adjust the paper so that the cutting line is where you want it. Holding the papers firmly, slide the cutting arm down. Now, separate the journaling box (or photo) and the mat. Move the pieces so the mat is even on all sides. Re-affix the journaling box (or photo) to the mat with several squares of double-sided tape.

How to Use Tip Boxes

Throughout this book, the Tip Boxes add value to the technique information. Read them in conjunction with the step-by-step how-to information on the same page.

About Those Time-Consuming Titles

Next to matting, the most complex and time-consuming part of most scrapbook pages is the page title or headline. With that in mind, this book starts by showing you how to use the quickest and easiest page titles and moves to more complex and time intensive headlines. The goal is to build your comfort level with a variety of page title methods. If possible, start with the simple and fast titles and move on sequentially as your confidence and abilities grow.

Fast Track Matting Tips

1. Use a personal trimmer with a replaceable sliding blade. If you work on 12" x 12" pages, buy a 12" trimmer.

2. Change your blade and rubber guide mat frequently. If your cuts look ragged, it may be the mat, not the blade.

3. Only use one square of double-sided tape to start. One square allows you to easily pull apart the journaling box (or photo) and the matting paper so you can adjust the spacing to make the outside margins of matting equal—even if you don't cut them equally.

4. If you can't see the cutting line (and it is hard to see), put a piece of white correction tape along the line.

5. If your matting paper is a large piece of paper, put the item to be matted in one of the corners so you only have to cut two sides.

SUPPLIES USED

Paper:
Frances Meyer

Page Topper:
Little Darlings, Almost
Homemade by
Amanda McLaws

Pens:
Avery and Zig

Other Supplies:
Personal Paper
Trimmer by Fiskars

? STORY STARTERS

What behaviors are typical of your child at different ages? Does she bite her nails? I'm a hair twirler, and my sister informed me I've been doing it since we were both little.

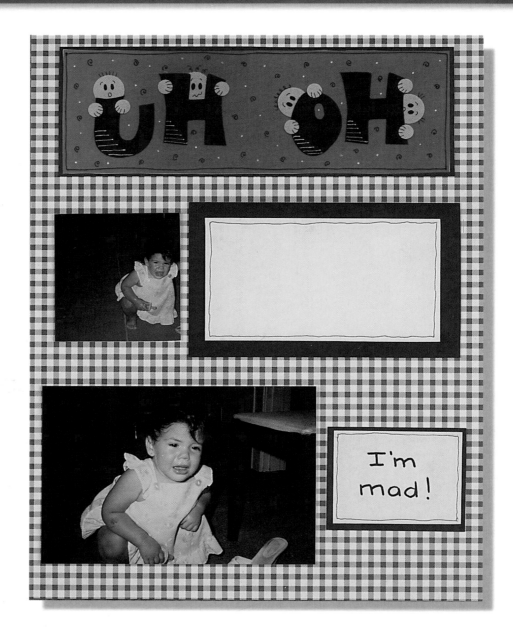

Good Golly, That Child Had a Temper

Looking at this page reminds me that my gorgeous, tall, teenage niece was once a toddler with a temper. Whatever set her off in these photos was probably minor. She would carry on like there was no tomorrow.

Notice that the page title says, "Uh-Oh." I could have used it for a boo-boo or an accident. With pre-printed material, use your imagination. Make pre-printed page elements work for you by figuring out how they fit the stories you want to save.

TECHNIQUE: *Using Pre-Printed Page Titles*

◀ Cut the page topper out of the page titles book or sheet. Trim around the outside edge. Mat the page topper onto black paper. Adhere it to the top of the page.

Cut a strip of plain white archival paper for your journaling boxes. Cut the strip into two pieces, one small and one larger. ▶

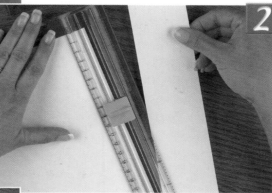

Sticky Stuff

In different situations, you'll want to use different archival adhesives.

Photo Splits or Photo Stickers: These are small squares of double-sided tape. They are best for holding big pieces of paper or photos.

Using these out of the box straight from the roll doesn't work for me. I take off the box and cut about a third of these in half. The small size works well for small places.

Roll-On Adhesive: This works well for medium-size items or intricately cut items.

Acid-Free Tape: You can fix torn photos or reinforce areas with this product. Primarily, it is used on the back side of a page where it doesn't show.

See the tip boxes on pages 11 and 41 for more insights on adhesives.

◀ Use an archival marker to draw a border inside the journaling boxes. The border does not have to be perfect! In fact, it looks better if you copy the wobbly line style of the page title's border.

Write in your caption with an archival pen. ▶

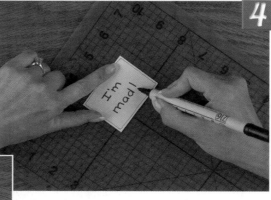

◀ Adhere your photos to the page. Mat both journaling boxes and adhere them to the page.

TOOLBOX

SUPPLIES USED

Paper:
Paper Pizazz

Page Topper:
PageTopper™, ©1999
by Cock-A-Doodle
Design, Inc.

Pens:
Zig and Avery

Dots:
Pop it-Up Dots

Other Supplies:
Personal Paper
Trimmer by Fiskars

? STORY STARTERS

*Yes, birthday parties
are great to scrapbook,
but life is also filled
with smaller, less fes-
tive celebrations.
Record the who, what,
when, where, why and
how of a lesser event.*

Yep, That's a Photo of Me Goofing Around

My pal Curt Hansen at Michigan Works! puts on the best administrative assistant conferences in the universe. When he asked me to be
the speaker at this conference, I jumped at the chance even though
it was held on my birthday. When the crowd sang to me, I acted pretty silly.
Is it a traditional celebration? No. Again, learn to make pre-printed materials
work for your stories. To heck with tradition. When I'm with conference at-
tendees I've known for years, it is a celebration. We've grown, learned and
changed together. That's worth a party any day.

TECHNIQUE: *Using Die Cuts*

◀ Mat your pre-printed page title. Cut a strip of white paper 2" x 3" for your journaling box. Mat your photos.

Lightly mark the dimensions of the ▶ journaling box and cut the box so that the mark is on the part of the paper you won't be using. This saves you from erasing your marks.

◀ Lay down all page elements and adhere them to the page. Add die cuts of streamers, making sure to overlap the elements.

To Crop or Not to Crop, That is the Question

Cropping is the term scrapbookers use for trimming a photo. Here are a few general rules:

1. Trim only a little at a time. (You can always cut off more later.)

2. Don't cut away backgrounds that later would bring back memories you want to remember, like the inside of your home.

3. Never crop old photos, photos for which you don't have a negative. Also, don't crop Polaroids because the white box at the bottom has chemicals in it.

4. Use a personal trimmer, as shown in these photos. It's the best way to get a straight parallel edge.

5. Don't use decorative edge scissors on photos. The edge design is distracting.

Tip!

Chalk It Up to Proper Shading

You can shade your die cuts and your paper with archival chalks. Although the chalks come with sponge applicators, I find it easier to use generic cotton swabs to apply chalk. The swabs are small, cheap and hold the right amount of chalk.

Where do you add the shading? You'll add darker colors where there are shadows and lighter colors where there are high points.

Feeling insecure? Flip your die cut over and color your shading in with a pencil first. If you don't like the result, erase your pencil shading and try again.

(You can erase chalk, but sometimes it's difficult.)

Another shading tip: Color from light to dark. It's easier to add color than to subtract it.

SUPPLIES USED

Paper & Die Cuts:
Quick & Easy
Scrapbook Page by
Pixie Press

Pens:
Zig and Avery

Dots:
Pop it-Up Dots

Other Supplies:
Personal Paper
Trimmer by Fiskars

? STORY STARTERS

Ever have a harrowing moment while on vacation? This photo was taken by the hotel security police.

I Don't Smoke, but My Carpet Did!

When room service wheeled in the cart with my breakfast, the lit can of Sterno underneath was knocked over. Instead of keeping my food warm, the Sterno leaked out onto my carpet.

I kept smelling smoke. Finally I stood up and looked underneath the cart. Since I was on the 47th Floor, I made an executive decision: Beat the flames out with my cloth napkin. Here's the burn mark that proves my bravery. (Spring 1999)

TECHNIQUE: *Creating a Photo Frame*

◄ Trim the patterned paper to create a strip 8 ½" x 5 ¼".

Make a pattern: Place tracing paper ► over your Polaroid. Trace the outline of the photo. Cut a window out of the tracing paper.

Make the frame: Set your photo on black paper and trace around its perimeter with a white pencil. Trim it.

◄ *Cut a window out of the frame*: Lay the tissue paper over the black paper frame. Trace the window with a white pencil. Cut out a window from the black paper. Center the frame over the photo. Use adhesive and adhere the frame to the photo.

Cut a playing card out of the patterned paper. Put a Pop-it Up Dot under the playing card and affix the card to one corner of your frame.

Outline your lettering with a pen. ►

◄ Build the page by adding elements to the background paper, working from the bottom up. Start with a caption box. Add the middle strip of patterned paper. Put on the page title. Adhere the matted photo and the matted journaling box to the patterned strip.

A HERMAfix Fix

My favorite adhesive is a brand called HERMAfix. I used this product on many of the pages in this book—which was really handy because I had to take them apart for the step-by-step photography.

You have to try HERMAfix to believe it. You can easily remove your items after adhering them, if you change your mind. Plus you can use a rubber eraser and remove the HERMAfix. Because the adhesive goes on as little dots, you can journal smoothly over paper backed with HERMAfix. (When your pen hits the bump caused by a photo split underneath your paper, your journaling can look weird.)

Of all the adhesives, HERMAfix product is the best bet for beginners and seasoned scrapbookers because you can easily detach an item or lift an edge to slip other elements underneath.

TOOLBOX

SUPPLIES USED

Lettering:
Letter Stickers from
Paper Adventures

Pen:
The Journaling Genie
Vanishing Ink Pen

Pencil:
Charcoal White by
General's

Other Supplies:
Two-Sided Craft Mat
by Fiskars

? STORY STARTERS

*Does your spouse still
participate in sports? If
so, what does he do
and how did he get
hooked on this activity?*

Hoop Star: David Slan Brings Home League Championship

David has been playing basketball since he was a youngster back in his hometown of Normal, Illinois. At that time, basketball star Doug Collins would come home to Normal and practice in the gym at University High School. Doug Collins would even play a bit with David and his pals. This photo was taken after David's JCCA team won their league championship. (Spring 2000)

TECHNIQUE: *Using Letter Stickers*

◀ Cut a strip of black paper 2 ¹/₂" x 8 ¹/₂". To mark the cut line on dark paper use a light or white colored pencil.

Cut a piece of patterned paper 2" x 7". Mark the cut line on heavily patterned paper by sticking a Post-it Note where you want to cut. ▶

◀ Cut a strip of white paper 1" x 8 ¹/₂" long. Use a pencil or The Journaling Genie Vanishing Ink Pen to mark the half-way point (at 4 ¹/₄"). Place the middle letters of your headline so that one is on each side of the mark. Continue, working from the center out.

Trim the right and left sides so that ▶ your finished headline paper is 5 ¹/₂" long. Center it and affix it to the matted page title box.
(NOTE: You could also start with a piece of paper 5 ¹/₂" long, but often bigger paper is easier to work with.)

◀ Cut a 2 ¹/₂" x 6" journaling box out of white paper. Attach it to a sheet of black paper and mat it. Mat your photo. Assemble the page.

Tip!

You'll Dream of Journaling Genie

You'll want to write "The Journaling Genie Vanishing Ink Pen by Chatterbox" on the top on your scrapbooking shopping list.

This miraculous pen leaves a pale pink mark on your paper that fades to nothing overnight if you leave your page out of the page protector. (I say miraculous with a smile because my son said, "Wow! How does it do that?")

If you don't have a Journaling Genie (JG) pen, you can use a pencil and simply erase your marks, but why waste the time?

Use the JG pen anytime you need to make a temporary mark on your scrapbook materials. You'll love it.

SUPPLIES USED

Paper:
Light Blue Linen by Keeping Memories Alive

Ice Cream Paper by Paper Pizazz

Letter Stickers:
Memories Forever

Line Stickers:
Mrs. Grossman's Design Line

Other Supplies:
Craft Knife by X-Acto

Have friends of your family welcomed your new additions in a unique way? What was it?

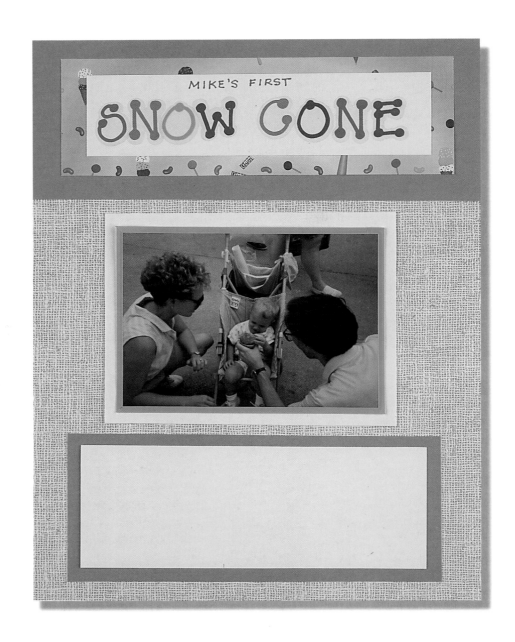

Mike's First Snow Cone

Michael was 25 months old (1991) the August that he and I visited his dad at the Illinois State Fair. The folks who ran the Lemon Shake-Up concession stand were longtime friends of ours.

They insisted it was time for Michael to try his first snow cone, on the house—er, on the booth. Michael wasn't sure about the treat at first, but it didn't take long to turn him into a lifelong snowcone fan.

TECHNIQUE: *Matting with Design Lines*

Crop your photo to 3 ¹/₂" x 5".

Cut from white paper:
  Journaling box: 2 ¹/₂" x 6 ¹/₂"
  Page title box: 1 ³/₄" by 6 ¹/₂"
  Photo mat: 4 ¹/₄" x 5 ¹/₂"

Cut from aqua paper:
  Journaling box mat: 3" x 7"

Assemble the journaling box and mat the photo.

Mark the halfway point on your page title box with a JG pen. Write in a small headline with the JG pen. If satisfied, go over the small headline with a marker.

Put the middle letter of the headline under the halfway mark on your headline box. (If you have an even number of letters, as I did, put one letter on each side of the halfway point.) Continue putting down letters working from the middle out.

Stretch Design Line sticker tape between your hands as shown. Press down one edge, laying the tape along the outside edge of the photo. Keep the tape taut. Press down the other end. Smooth the tape along the photo's edge. Repeat on all sides.

Set the craft knife blade at a 45° angle where the tapes intersect. Press down to cut. NOTE: Don't let the blade extend beyond the inside tape edge. Peel away the excess. Repeat on all corners. Attach all elements to the page.

Using Letter Stickers

Letter stickers go on fast and give you polished results.

Here are a few tips:

1. Keep your headlines short—You'll save space, aggravation and money on stickers.

2. Stickers on clear backgrounds seem to tear at the perforations. Keep your craft knife ready to cut the letters from the backing.

3. The simpler the lettering style the more useful the stickers will be.

4. Run out of the letters you need? Use a zero for an O and a 3 for an E. Try a 7 for an L or cut off one part of the letter T. Cut off part of an R or a B to make a P. Slice into a G to create a C. An M upside down is a W.

TOOLBOX

SUPPLIES USED

Paper:
The Paper Patch

Lettering:
Letter Stickers from
Paper Adventures

Other Supplies:
Therm O Web Acid-
Free Self-Adhesive
Laminate, from Keep
a Memory

Mrs. Grossman's
Design Lines

? STORY STARTERS

*Food packaging tells so
much. We see nutrition
fads, taste trends and
graphic preferences.
Write about a food
your family eats with
pleasure.*

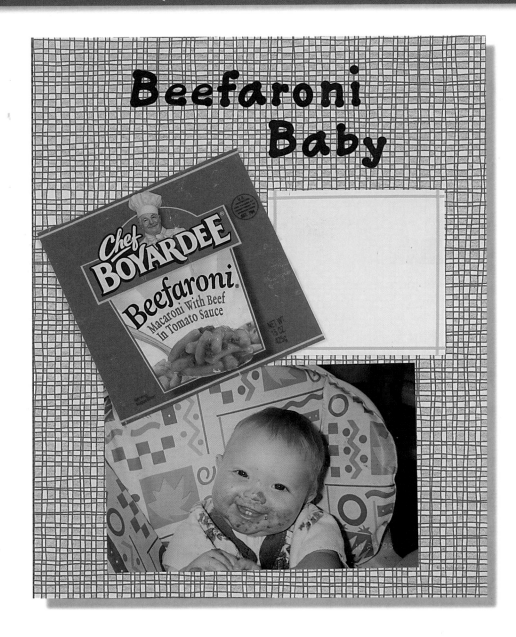

Beefaroni Baby–She's Having Beefaroni All Over!

This baby wanted to eat "big people" food from Day One. Oh, how Renee would stare at our plates and howl! She knew baby food was blah, blah, blah, but would we fork over the regular chow? NO! Once Margaret introduced her to regular food, Renee was an eager eater. Some of the food actually made it into her mouth. As you can see, Beefaroni is as fun to wear as it is to eat.

TECHNIQUE: *Using Laminate Film*

◀ Use the item you wish to laminate as a pattern and trace around it on the paper side of the laminate film. Cut a piece of film 1/2" larger than your pattern on all sides. Peel the backing off and stick down one corner, continuing to peel and smoothing down. Repeat on the reverse side of the item.

Cut a white journaling box 3 1/4" x ▶ 3 1/4". Starting 1/4" in and at the top of one edge, run Design Line sticker tape down one side. Repeat this on all sides. Trim off the excess.

◀ Measure to the mid-point of the page and mark it with a Post-it Note. Count the letters in the title. Align the middle letter of the title with the mid-point of the page. Stick down the letters, working from the middle to the outside. Adhere all the elements to the page.

Don't Lament— Laminate

There's so much you can do with this easy-to-use archival laminate film. Covering a page element with this film safeguards your photos from migrating acid. Here are a few things you might want to "laminate":

- Food labels
- Recipe cards
- Magazine articles
- Newspaper articles
- Programs
- Greeting cards
- Report cards
- Tickets
- Certificates
- School assignments
- Grocery lists
- Coloring book pages
- Art projects
- Food box fronts
- Labels from toy packaging
- Instructions
- Playing cards
- Cartoons

It's also great for protecting the covers of soft-bound books.

A Quick Primer on Archivally Safe Products

Over time, your photos can be destroyed by acid that migrates from your hands and other products. To safeguard your photos, only use paper and products that meet archival standards. For the most part, you'll have to trust the product packaging. However, a more reliable guide to product safety is the CK OK, which guarantees that the product has passed rigorous third-party testing to verify its safety.

The purpose of the laminate film described above is to contain the acid found in the paper and ink of the label. Lamination of any kind is not recommended for your photos. You could also spray the label with a deacidifying spray available from your scrapbook store.

SUPPLIES USED

Paper:
Keeping Memories Alive

Pencil:
Berol

Pen:
Zig

Lettering:
Frances Meyer template for letters

Stickers:
© 1995, 1996 and 1998 Nintendo

Other Supplies:
© 1995, 1996 and 1998 Nintendo

Carlton Cards Sticker Station

Craft Knife by X-Acto

? STORY STARTERS

What national playtime fads are your children addicted to? Ever go to a convention to seek out new play things? What was it like?

Pokemon Trading: It's a Mad, Mad World

When a local mall advertised Pokemon Trading on a Saturday, Michael couldn't wait to go. The place was a mad house with thousands and thousands of kids.

It turned out that the event was not at all what had been promised, so Michael got a lesson in deceptive advertising. He also learned the vagaries of setting value with some kids being clueless and others being unreasonable. (Spring 2000)

TECHNIQUES: *Using a Letter Template & Creating Page Corners with Stickers*

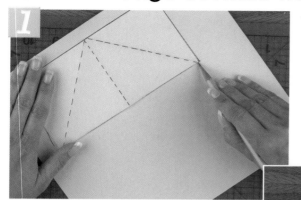

◀ Trace the outside edge of the pattern (found in the Templates section at www.scrapbookstorytelling.com) onto a piece of solid or tracing paper, leaving 1/2" on all sides. Or, photocopy and enlarge the Pokémon page to use as a pattern.

Apply the stickers to the rectangle drawn on the solid paper. Overlap the stickers so they extend off the edge. With a craft knife, cut off the overhanging stickers. Adhere the cut pieces to the rectangle with the sticker edge against the outline edge of the rectangle. Cut all four corners. ▶

◀ Cut a strip of paper 1 3/4" x 6". Mark the mid-point of the paper at 3". Put the lettering template on the paper and trace the middle letter in pencil. Trace the other letters working from the middle out. Color in the letters. Outline the letters with a marker.

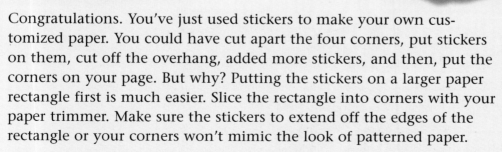

Pikachu in the Corner Pocket— A Simple Layout Trick

Congratulations. You've just used stickers to make your own customized paper. You could have cut apart the four corners, put stickers on them, cut off the overhang, added more stickers, and then, put the corners on your page. But why? Putting the stickers on a larger paper rectangle first is much easier. Slice the rectangle into corners with your paper trimmer. Make sure the stickers to extend off the edges of the rectangle or your corners won't mimic the look of patterned paper.

Of course, you can use this same layout technique with any stickers. Even small stickers grouped together can have visual impact. If you use patterned paper for your background, make sure the pattern doesn't compete with your custom sticker corners.

SUPPLIES USED

Paper:
The Paper Center

Stickers:
Hallmark

? STORY STARTERS

Babysitters have been important in our family life. Document who these key people are, and why your family appreciates them.

All God's Children Need a Place to Call Home...

Erin Vonesh, fourth from the left, is Michael's swimming instructor and was his babysitter until she went to college. Now her brother Pat, first from left, comes over when my husband and I go out for a date.

Here are the Voneshes and the Ascension Youth Group as they took off for Fort Smith, Arkansas, on the Fourth of July, 1998, to spend their holiday working with Habitat for Humanity.

TECHNIQUE: *Using Imprintable Paper*

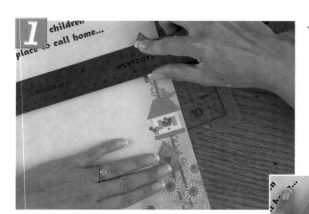

◀ Measure the left and right border on your imprintable (or stationery). Set the margins on your computer accordingly. Print your headline on a piece of waste paper and make spacing adjustments. Print a final version of your headline directly on the imprintable paper.

Add a strip of white paper that is pre-cut to fit for your journaling. Crop and mat your photo so that the imprintable's border will slightly overlap the mat. Use a craft knife to cut along the inside edge of the border elements. ▶

◀ Slip a matted photo beneath the border elements. Adjust it so the photo is straight. Adhere it with photo splits under the top and bottom. Use document-safe tape on the back of the page to secure the matted photo.

Imprintables: You Know It as Stationery

You'll recognize this paper as what you've seen in quick print shops, stationery shops, party and office supply stores. The center is left blank for your message, which makes these paper products perfect for simple scrapbook layouts. Use it for:

- **Borders**—As is, or cut out and adhered to other paper.
- **Embellishments**—Cut out design elements.
- **Journaling boxes**—Use postcards or fold-over notes.
- **Pockets**—Use extra envelopes or buy them separately.
- **Frames**—Mat your photo in the center.

Tip!

Getting the Spacing Just Right on Your Computer

Here are three ways to be sure your spacing is correct:

1. Hold the stationery and the computer generated copy up to the light or put it on a light table. You should be able to see through the sheets. Adjust spacing accordingly.

2. Photocopy or scan the stationery. Print out the computer generated type on the photocopy. Don't print on the "good" paper until you are satisfied with your results.

3. If you don't mind wasting paper, simply print out the headline on the stationery the first time, adjust the spacing and re-print it on another sheet.

TOOLBOX

SUPPLIES USED

Paper:
Velour Craft Paper by Hygloss

Easter Paper by The Paper Patch

Lettering:
Letter Stickers by Paper Adventures

Pen:
Micron Pen by Sakura

Chalks:
Decorating Chalks by Craft-T Products

Other Supplies:
Tracing Paper

? STORY STARTERS

What was your child's reaction to an adult in costume? Children's responses vary from delight to horror. How did the kids in your family respond?

Lexie, Our Honey, and That Old Easter Bunny

Ever since she was born, Lexie has been a natural in front of the camera. It's not her style to miss a photo opportunity. Unlike some kids who get scared by people dressed as holiday figures, Lexie never balked. Here she is at Southlake Mall, Indiana, 1987.

Note that lovely long hair. It was short until age two and then, we had a budding Rapunzel on our hands.

TECHNIQUE: *Making a Design Transfer*

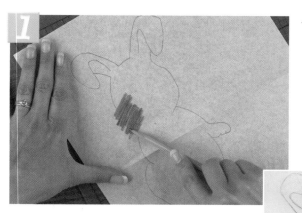

◄ Make a copy of the rabbit template (found in the Templates section at www.scrapbookstorytelling.com). Or, photocopy and enlarge the Easter Bunny page to use as a pattern. Flip the copy over. On the back, color along the design with a pencil. You are laying down carbon for a later transfer of a design.

When finished coloring on the back, flip the paper over again. Trace the design onto velour paper with a slightly dull pencil. The pressure of the pencil will transfer the carbon image to the velour paper. ▶

◄ Cut out the rabbit. Use markers and chalk to color in the features. Mat a 2 $1/4$" x 3 $1/2$" white box for your headline. Mark the midpoint (1 $3/4$") and lay down the letter stickers. Mat your photo and journaling boxes as desired. Add all the elements to the page.

Design Transfer Tips

1. Re-trace your pattern with a black felt tip marker to help it show up.

2. You don't need to color in the whole back of the pattern, but you **must** have carbon directly behind the design. Periodically, hold your paper to the light or use a light box to check your coloring progress.

3. To lay down more carbon, cross hatch your pencil strokes. Color from lower left to upper right, then from upper left to lower right.

4. Before flipping the paper over, run a tissue over the carbon to pick up excess carbon and to avoid smudging the "good" paper.

5. When transferring to dark paper, use a white or light pencil. White carbon pencils are available at your local craft or art supply store.

6. When tracing over your pattern to deposit the carbon, tape down both sheets of paper (pattern and "good" paper) to avoid slippage.

Making a Pattern with an Overhead Transparency

If you plan to use a pattern several times, you may wish to make an overhead transparency pattern rather than do a design transfer each time. Here's how:

• Copy the template onto an overhead transparency. (Buy these at an office supply store and run them through a photocopier or go to a copy shop and ask them to make a transparency for you at a minimal price.)

• Label the transparency pattern parts with a permanent marker.

• Cut them apart to use as pattern pieces, but keep the original copy to help you assemble the pieces.

• Store the copy and the pieces in a plastic bag.

TOOLBOX

SUPPLIES USED

Paper:
Water paper by
Memories Forever

Metallic paper by
Hygloss

Markers:
Zig

Pen:
Marvy

Pencil:
Berol

Other Supplies:
Tracing Paper

? STORY STARTERS

What does your child want to be? What did YOU want to be? What influenced your thinking?

When I Grow Up, I Want to be a Fireman. Maybe...

At a neighborhood get-together, the local fire department passed out safety literature and took Polaroids of kids in fire fighting gear.

Michael was gung ho until all the gear was on. Then the full weight was so staggering that he struggled to keep a brave face. He was barely balanced for this photo. (Summer 1992, Champaign, Illinois)

TECHNIQUE: *Practicing Paper Piecing Skills*

◄ Use the design transfer method or the pattern method (see page 23) to transfer the Dalmation pup (templates at www.scrapbookstorytelling.com) to white paper. Transfer his hat to red paper. Transfer the nozzle and hat emblem to metallic or gold-colored paper. Add the details and cut out.

Use the design transfer method with a white pencil or the pattern method to transfer the fire hose to black paper. Add a nozzle to the hose with half of a square of double stick tape. ►

◄ Use the design transfer method to create water spray. Cut the spray from light blue paper. Re-trim the spray with deckle scissors. Journal on the water spray. Add it to the nozzle. Add all the elements to the page, tucking the photo inside the dog paw and securing it with squares of double-sided tape.

Small Image, Big Impact

Polaroids such as this one and the one of the Easter Bunny on page 22 can be a design challenge because the image in the photo is small. Instead of focusing on the small image, take your cue from the occasion. By paper piecing a large embellishment, you draw the focus to the photo. Best of all, you can have fun by creating a large embellishment like the bunny or the dog.

These pages work in part because of the rule of thirds. To have visual impact, one image or color must dominate roughly 2/3 of the page.

Become an Alterations Expert

Be creative with the templates in this book. There's nothing sacred about them. Sparky, in this incarnation, is a Dalmation. But, with curly white fur, he's a Bichon Frise or a poodle. With curly white and black or brown fur, he's a spaniel. A blonde Sparky is a golden retriever. Add brown, white and black spots and Sparky admits to his beagle blood.

Try new expressions of a template. First cover your original pattern with tissue paper. Trace the old lines you want to keep. Now, sketch in the new features. If you have a picture of what you are aiming for, so much the better. Remember your eraser and your imagination, and dump that little voice that cries, "Hey, you're no Rembrandt!" See something you like? Copy it with a marker and use it for a pattern.

Other Patterns

Need other simple patterns for paper piecing? Take a look at coloring books!

TOOLBOX

SUPPLIES USED

Paper:
Vellum paper

Punch:
Circle punch by Marvy

Adhesive:
Neutral pH Adhesive by
Lineco Inc.

Other Supplies:
Circle Cutter by Fiskars

? STORY STARTERS

Life is filled with first times. First bubbles, first whistles, first bike rides without training pedals, first airplane flight, and so on. Share how your child mastered the skill or situation.

He's Forever Blowing Bubbles

Well, he huffed and he puffed and he spit wads of gum all over the place. Then one magical day it appeared—a bubble! Michael was so excited he wrote "6-14-99 First Bubble" on the unfinished inside garage wall we use for special announcements. Since then, he's mastered the art of blowing a bubble within a bubble. Our new challenge is getting those burst bubbles off his face.

TECHNIQUE: *Working with Vellum*

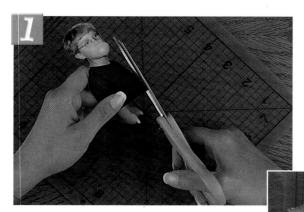

◀ If you aren't entirely happy with the background in your photo, do a silhouette crop. Cut away the background leaving a tiny edge around the subject of your photo.

Use a circle cutter to cut a white circle 5 $1/4$" in diameter and a mauve circle 5 $1/2$" in diameter. Write your journaling in the white circle and affix it to the mauve mat. ▶

◀ Cut a white headline box 1 $1/2$" x 3 $1/2$". Write the headline. Mat the box in mauve. Using a 1 $3/4$" circle punch, punch out seven circles of white paper and seven circles of white vellum. Lay letter stickers on each white circle. Overlap the letter circles using archival glue. Mat the combined circles in mauve.

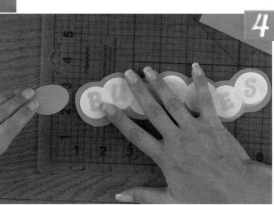

Use a small dab of archival glue in the upper right side of each vellum circle to attach the vellum circle to the paper circle. ▶

Add a shading of pink chalk to the upper right side of the vellum. Attach the headline box to the "Bubbles." Affix all the elements to the page.

A Thin Veil of Vellum

Vellum creates a useful sheer illusion for your pages. But, because it is sheer, most glues show through. You can:

- Attach vellum by tying it on with a ribbon or piece of raffia run through holes at the top.
- Overlap the vellum using opaque paper both as a frame or as an embellishment to hold the vellum down.
- Use a solid sheet adhesive such as Xyron or Keep a Memory Mounting Adhesive.
- Hide your adhesive behind a shaded, colored, or computer printed area on the vellum. The shading of the bubbles hides the glue effectively on this page.

? STORY STARTERS

What the school shares is worthy, but your child's reaction to the program is even more fascinating. Talk about the preparation, the actual event and the comments after the fact.

All School Program at Chesterfield Day School, St. Albans

Michael practiced and practiced his jump rope program. Then his German teacher asked him to accompany his class on the keyboard. All in all, this evening program was the culmination of many weeks of effort at home and at school.

I loved Michael's pride in his accomplishments and in the efforts of his fellow students. Here he waits his turn while watching the younger grades perform. (Spring 2000)

TECHNIQUE: *Tackling Advanced Paper Piecing*

◀ Make several copies of your paper pattern.* Cut the pieces apart and use HERMAfix to temporarily adhere them to the paper. Cut out the desk using the pattern. Adhere the photo inside the desk. Cut out a blackboard using the pattern. Cut out a pencil cup using the pattern.

Cut a strip of white paper $5/8$" wide ▶ and 8" long. Use HERMAfix to secure the strip immediately under the alphabet on the pattern. Recopy the alphabet onto white paper using the pattern as a guide. Attach it to the top of the page.

◀ Put HERMAfix on the back of wood grained paper. Use a paper trimmer to make the strips $1/4$" wide. Attach the strips to the blackboard and miter the corners as explained on page 15.

Cut strips of yellow paper $3/8$" wide ▶ and 1 $1/2$" long. Use a gold metallic ink pen to color in the metal band at the top of the pencil. Glue the pencil to pink paper and cut out the eraser tip.

* See scrapbookstorytelling.com for more information on this template.

Cutting Thin Strips of Paper

If you add stripes of HERMAfix to the back of your paper, you can easily cut out thin strips of paper without having them slip around. Use a craft knife to peel the thin strips off the personal trimmer.

Customizing a Kit

Schoolmates by Mountains of Memories is a cute paper piecing kit. But, this photo of my son had a busy and important background. So, I used only selected parts of the kit to simplify the page and to focus on my photo.

Remember: Kits are tools, not rules. Don't be hesitant to add or subtract from the materials you've purchased.

White Writing

You could journal with a white pencil to look like chalk on the blackboard. Try it!

OUR FAMILY

STORY STARTERS

I love seeing family photos and noticing how people change. The styles, the relationships, the losses and additions are all a part of our history.

TOOLBOX

SUPPLIES USED

Paper:	Wallpaper: BABS–Building a Better Scrapbook
	Wood: Provo Craft
	Stained glass: Paper Pizazz
	Metallic paper: Hygloss
Stickers:	Lace: Annette Allen Watkins Printworks
	Frames: Frances Meyer
	Letters: Memories Forever

A Great Idea from the Heart of Texas

I was visiting San Antonio, Texas, when I stopped by Scrapbooks from the Heart. I met the owner Sharon Capshaw and her ace helper Lisa Elsik. Lisa showed me a page like this. I sketched it in my notebook and made it two years later. The point? Always carry paper and pen with you. You never know when you'll see a great idea. Even if you don't get to it right away, you'll have it when you're ready.

While there's plenty of room for a journaling box, I like using a page like this for all photos that are too small for most scrapbook spreads.

TECHNIQUE: *Creating a Tableau*

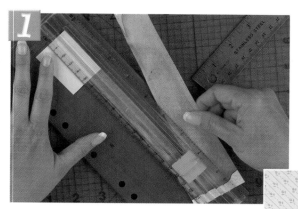

◄ *Create a table*: Cut two strips of wood patterned paper each 1 1/2" x 6 1/2" to form a table top. Cut two more strips 3/4" wide and 1 1/2" long for the legs.

Assemble the table: Start 3" from the bottom of the page, and adhere the table top on the left and right sides. You'll have 1 1/2" of open area below the table. Add the legs, slipping them in 3/4" from the right edge of the table and 3/4" from the left edge. ►

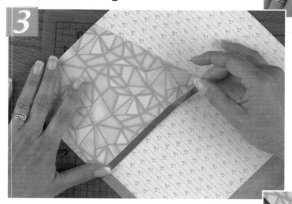

◄ *Create a Tiffany lamp*: Use the lamp pattern from www.scrapbookstorytelling.com. Adhere the left and right pieces of the shade starting from the top. Cut out the lamp stand and attach it. Put strips of adhesive on the back of the metallic paper and cut it into two 1/4" x 6" strips. Affix the strips to the bottom of the lamp shade.

Make a table skirt: Cut two strips of ► white vellum 2" x 5 1/2". Place the vellum on top of the table, hanging down. Add a strip of lace sticker across the bottom and on the right and left side to hold the vellum. Add the photos in the frame stickers.

◄ The bottom of your photo frame stickers will help hold the vellum to the page.

Peel off sticker letters and press them down for a headline.

It's a Frame Up

You already know how to frame these photos. Use tissue paper to trace the frame like we did on page 11. That way you'll know if your photo will fit inside. If the frame will work, peel off the sticker and put it over your image. THEN cut off any of the photo that sticks out past the frame.

Need a Bigger Frame?

Leave the waxy backing on these stickers and cut apart two frames. Be sure to cut along a design. Then piece the frames back together so you have the perimeter of two frames instead of one. Add photo safe tape to the back to join the pieces. Peel off backing and apply the sticker.

Why cut along a design? Your eye follows the lines of the design and your cut marks are much less noticeable.

? STORY STARTERS

What historic site near your home do you keep intending to visit? Go there and record your trip.

SUPPLIES USED

Paper:	Keeping Memories Alive
Stickers:	Floral stickers by Mrs. Grossman's
Lettering:	Log Letters by Provo Craft
Pen:	Metallic Gel Roller by Marvy
Other Supplies:	Photo & Document Mending Tape by 3M

The Bacon Log Cabin: A Local Landmark

On our way to Michael's friend Chris Helm's house, we often passed the historical marker for the Bacon Log Cabin. One day I decided it was silly to keep passing this place by and not visit. So we stopped. It was early Spring 2000 and the irises were in full splendor. Michael, Kevin and I wandered around and marveled at the old log construction, still sturdy after nearly 100 years. So often when a special place is nearby, we never visit. We wait for visitors or simply put off going. I'm determined to stop more often and smell the irises.

TECHNIQUE: *Working with Double Page Spreads*

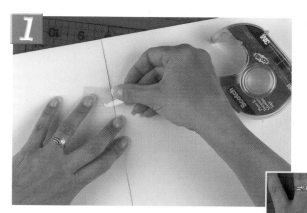

◄ Turn the background pages over and abut them. Put a piece of tape on the back toward the top to secure the pages. Repeat closer to the bottom of the pages. Flip the pages over to work on them as one unit.

Cut a strip of lavender paper 2" x 9 ¹/2". With a JG pen, write in a headline. Go over it with a marker. Use letter stickers for capitals. Add flower stickers to the capitals. Add Design Line sticker tape to the top and bottom. ►

◄ Mat all the photos. Crop and mat a journaling box. Affix the page title to the top of the page with numerous squares of double-sided tape. Add photos. Turn the page upside down and use a personal trimmer to cut it apart into two pages.

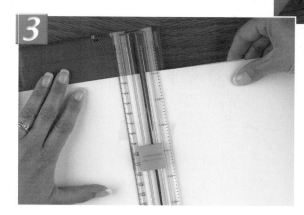

Tip!

The Joy of Overlapping

Every time you pause to crop a photo, you use precious scrapbooking time. That's fine, if the photo needs to be cropped. But so often, all you need to do is overlap a small portion of the photo for the same space-saving results.

As a bonus, overlapping of photos—or any design elements—causes the eye to flow more easily from one image to another.

For best results:

- Experiment with your photos to decide which one looks best on top and which is best partially covered (see page 34 for an example).

- Try letting design elements like borders, page titles, page corners and die cuts overlap your photos. (See page 18 for an example.)

Key Considerations of Double Page Spreads

Double page spreads are a terrific way to tell stories in your scrapbook. The problem for most scrappers is that they work on the pages separately, so they never quite look right side by side. By taping the two papers together, you see them as one page. You treat them as one page. You can't help but end up with a coherent visual image. A few more tips:

- Position page titles so they split between words, not between letters.

- If you decide to split a photo, try to have at least 2/3 on one side and 1/3 on the other. Half and half usually doesn't work.

- Cut the pages apart with a fresh blade on your personal trimmer.

- You can store both pages side by side in a panorama page protector.

? STORY STARTERS

Taking photos of the animals is fun, but your child's changing reaction to the place is even more interesting. As a child matures, his or her interests change. Record those changes.

The St. Louis Zoo is Zoo-Pendous!

The first nice weekend in the Spring of 2000 we took a family trip to the St. Louis Zoo. Five years ago, a baby elephant was born here. As Raja has grown, the zoo has needed to improve his living area. The result is a beautiful, natural space called the River's Edge.

When we first moved here, all Michael wanted to do at the zoo was ride the train. As he has grown, he's become interested in the displays of animals and insects.

TECHNIQUE: *Using Kit Elements on Double Pages*

◀ Cut out design elements and a page title from a page of printed pieces. Cut off the monkey attached to the branch. (His hands barely show in the final page layout.) Flip the pages over and tape them together on the back side.

Use an oval cropper to crop at least ▶ three photos. Use fine sanding paper or a fingernail sanding block to smooth them. Crop other photos as desired or into approximate shapes as shown. Create a journaling box of 3 ¹/2" x 4".

◀ Arrange the elements on the page and adhere. Overlap the oval photos and the rectangular photo on the right page. Use a craft knife to lift up the branch and slide the elephant slightly beneath it. Let the leaves on the branch at the page bottom overlap the photos.

Using Oval and Circle Cutters

Back in the old days of scrapbooking, circle cutters were heavy contraptions you used with a piece of glass underneath. Today, they are lighter, easier to use, and much less expensive. A few thoughts:

- Buy an oval or circle cutter with a blade you can replace easily. If you can't buy replacement blades, you can't use the cutter for long.

- Practice, practice, practice. Use spare, out of focus or discardable photos for this. Photographic paper is a different thickness than other paper, so practicing on real photos will teach you a lot.

- After you set the size, cut a circle or oval out of waste paper. Hold it over your photo to make sure you have the size you want.

Tip!

You're Looking Very Buff, Ms. Oval

No matter how careful you are, your ovals and circles will probably have a few bumps and lumps. If you try to even this out with scissors, you'll have a disaster on your hands.

I once whittled a photo down to the size of a dime, but by golly, it was a perfectly circular dime once I finished with that rascal. Instead of reaching for the blades, grab a piece of fine sanding paper or a fingernail sanding block, sometimes called a buffing block.

Sand off those rough edges. Since these edges aren't fingernails, you can and should rub back and forth to get a smooth edge. If your finished edge looks white, hold a dark marker parallel to the edge and color it in.

SUPPLIES USED

Paper:
Paper Pizazz

Stickers:
Mrs. Grossman's
Design Lines

Chalk:
Decorating Chalk by
Craft-T Products

Punches:
Circle punch by Marvy

Reindeer punch by
Family Treasures

? STORY STARTERS

*What holiday activities
do you share with other
families? Why are those
families important to
you?*

Visit www.scrapbookstorytelling.com for variations
on this layout.

Feeding Santa's Reindeer: Christmas, 1999

Since my friend Elaine's children are three and six years younger than
my son, they give me a second chance for fun with youngsters. When
I saw the recipe for reindeer food, I knew Daniele and Alexandre
would think this pet chow was "way cool." Although the weather was more
dreary than Christmasy, the children had a festive time on this December
night.

TECHNIQUE: *Combining a Variety of Techniques*

◀ Cut a square of patterned paper 3 ¹/2" x 3 ¹/2". Cut that square diagonally to create two triangles for your corners. Add Design Line sticker tape. Cut a white journaling box 3 ³/4" x 4 ¹/4." Cut another journaling box 4 ¹/2" x 5 ¹/4". Prepare a 5" x 5" piece of green paper to mat the smaller white box later.

The Stuff Between the Pop-it Up Dots Comes to the Rescue

These reindeer had to fly. But the Pop-it Up Dots were too big for these punch pieces. So, I used the area usually tossed away that falls between the dots.

Double mat one photo with solid green and patterned paper. Silhouette crop one photo. Crop one photo to 3 ¹/4" x 4". Use a sponge paint brush to stroke black chalk across the top of the small white journaling box. Add more chalk to make it look like a dark sky. ▶

◀ Punch three reindeer from black paper. Punch a yellow circle with a 1 ³/4" circle punch. Glue the circle to the upper right corner of the small journaling box. Cut small pieces of Pop-it Up Dots and put them under the reindeer and add them to the box. Mat the box with 5" x 5" green paper. Add the reindeer to the page. Assemble all the elements on the page.

Black Christmas Paper?

Paper addicts of the scrapbooking world unite! You can never, ever, ever have too much paper. Repeat after me: I can never, ever, ever have too much paper.

Combinations of Techniques Make for Great Pages

Once you master a technique, you tend to use that new found ability over and over. Once in a while, challenge yourself to combine techniques to effectively tell your stories on the pages. Here we have punch art, chalk, Design Line border, corner embellishment, Pop-it Up Dots, silhouette cropping and overlapping. A real duke's mixture, as my mom would say.

Now for the contradiction: Reuse successful layouts as often as possible. By changing the color scheme, and the punch art, this page can be remodeled to tell many stories. Check out scrapbookstorytelling.com for an example.

Never Pass Up a Sale on Solid Paper

It looks a little plain sitting there in the store. Big deal. Solids are the plain black pumps of scrapbooking. You can't build a great look without them.

? STORY STARTERS

Once in a while, an un-planned opportunity for fun crosses our paths. How did you partici-pate?

TOOLBOX

SUPPLIES USED

Punch: Swirl punch by Family Treasures
Lettering: Die cut lettering by Ellison

Fun at the Carnival in Vincennes

*O*ur trips to Vincennes, Indiana, to see Grandma Marge were pretty bor-ing for an active guy like Michael. When we spotted the carnival, we were elated. Michael quickly sized up the games and figured out which ones offered the best prospects for winning. Because the skies were overcast, we didn't have to compete with any crowds, and Michael could play his favorite games over and over. (Spring 1999)

TECHNIQUE: *Creating a Background with Punch Art*

◄ Flip over two sheets of paper and tape them together on the back side. Using a spiral punch, punch out curls in an assortment of colors. Turn the punch upside down for precise placement. Cut a strip of green paper 1 $3/4$" x 8". Cut a white 3" x 4" journaling box.

Lightly trace where your photos will go with a pencil. Glue down the spirals. A few should extend into where the photos will go, but you don't need to fill the spaces behind the photos. ►

◄ Affix die cut letters to the green strip of paper. Position the green banner so that the page split falls between letters. Adhere the page title to the pages. Affix all elements to the page. Use a personal trimmer to cut the two pages apart.

Die Cut Lettering—An Easy Option

If you are lucky enough to have access to a die cut machine, crank out those letters! You can also buy die cut letters in scrapbook or craft stores.

The difficulty is knowing in advance which and how many letters you might need. If your scrapbooking store rents time on a die cut machine, you might want to do what the letter sticker people do and make multiples of common letters. I suggest these quantities:

- 5 of the letters A, E, I, O, U
- 4 of L, N, S and T
- 3 of B, C, D, F, G, H, J, K, M, P, and R
- 2 of Q, V, W, and Y
- 1 of X and Z

Of course, if you have a family member with a name like JeNNifer or SaLLy, you might want to add an extra of that doubled letter.

A Collection of Miscellaneous Tips

- Don't waste time or supplies on areas that will be covered by photos.

- Patronize scrapbooking retailers who offer discounts to frequent buyers.

- Use the equipment at stores and at crops before you invest in tools for yourself. You may decide you don't like using a particular tool, so why get stuck with it?

- A subscription or two to scrapbooking magazines is well worth the money. You'll get great ideas, inspiration, how to's, and news on new products.

- Only keep scraps of paper big enough to punch.

- Get organized. It maximizes the time you can spend on pages.

TOOLBOX

SUPPLIES USED

Paper:
Plain blue

Happy New Year
Vellum by Bits & Pieces

? STORY STARTERS

The holidays are always noteworthy but special circumstances such as the beginning of a millennium deserve particular attention. What did your family do to mark the occasion?

Happy New Year!

The Year 2000 began on the Sabbath. To mark this wonderfully auspicious change of dates, we first lit the candles, drank the wine (grape juice for Michael) and ate the challah, thanking God for all His blessings. Then we put on party hats and endured Michael blowing noisemakers until we had all the happiness we could stand.

TECHNIQUE: *Using a Vellum Page Title*

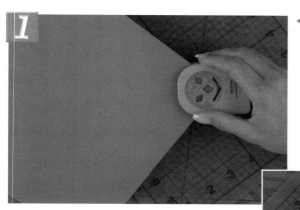

◀ Turning your punch upside down for precise placement, punch out diamonds in a variety of colors. Trace where photos will go on your pages. Affix punch art, extending some pieces where the photos are going, but not trying to cover the entire photo space.

Color in your vellum page title with markers or colored pencils. Color in the smallest areas first, and then move to larger areas. ▶

◀ Cut a journaling box 2 1/2" x 5 3/4". Affix the vellum box to the page with diamonds. Part of the diamonds will be glued to the vellum and part to the page. Affix all elements to the page.

Not All Preprinted Vellum is Created Equal

This page features vellum lettering by the talented and creative Robin Johnson of Bits & Pieces. If you look carefully at preprinted vellum, you'll see that many brands don't use high quality printing like Robin does.

Glue Sticks and Glue Pens

To glue down small punch pieces like these and the curls on the previous page, try these products:

• 2 Way Glue by Zig

• Acid-free Photo-Safe glue stick by Avery

• Neutral pH Adhesive by Lineco Inc. Use a toothpick to apply this glue.

Page Title Lettering Options: An Overview

Vellum preprinted—These pages titles have flexibility of color but not of the wording or the size.

Die cut and sticker lettering—This lettering gives flexibility of color, style and size with total control of the wording.

Letter stenciling or letter templates—Stencils and templates are sold in many sizes and styles and give total control of color and wording.

Preprinted page titles—Flexibility of size and saying at purchase.

Computer printed— Unlimited flexibility of size, color and style and total control of the wording.

Hand lettering—Ultimate control over all variables.

Uncolored letter stickers—These stickers are available in many sizes and styles and give you total control of color and wording.

TOOLBOX

SUPPLIES USED

Paper:
Background paper:
Keeping Memories
Alive

Baseball journaling
piece: Notes & Quotes
by Scrap-Ease, © 1998
What's New, Ltd.

Pens:
Marvy LePlume

Other Supplies:
Circle cutter by Fiskars

? STORY STARTERS

*Catch your favorite ball
player in action. Write
about what your family
members enjoyed and
disliked about team
sports.*

Batter Up!

The coach of Michael's baseball team described the Summer 1999 season as "character building." That was a euphemism for "the pits." The team only won one game all summer.

Michael displayed a great wiggle and sense of theatre at bat. But after seeing so many kids clobbered by wildly pitched balls, he was not an enthusiastic player. Who could blame him?

TECHNIQUE: *Matting a Bump Crop*

◀ Use your JG pen to mark how much space you have for the words in your page title. Trace the letters with the JG pen, slightly overlapping them. If satisfied, re-copy the letters with a pumpkin colored pencil. Color in the letters and re-trace the outlines with a black marker.

Trace a wavy border around the lettering area with a JG pen. Go over the border using a marker. Cut out the headline. ▶

Cut the journaling embellishment out of the embellishments page. Cut the journaling box 2" x 6 ¹/2".

◀ Use an oval cropper on the photo you wish to bump crop, but do NOT cut a complete oval. Instead, start in front of the area you wish to bump out and stop your blade slightly behind the area you wish to bump out. Use scissors to complete the bump crop. Attach the headline, journaling box and bump photo to a piece of paper 7" x 11". Outline the mat, allowing for a bump, using a JG pen. Cut. Affix all elements to the page.

Undo with un-du

On your next shopping trip, grab a bottle of this solvent.

Un-du loosens adhesives so that you can easily peel off double-stick tape or stickers without ripping your paper.

Also use un-du to:

• Wipe off ink from plastic.

• Remove excess adhesive that sticks out from behind an item.

• Remove gummy residue left behind by a label.

• Open envelope flaps.

• Remove tape.

All you need is one mistake, and a bottle of un-du pays for itself. Rather than trash an entire page because of a goof, use your un-du and start over. Every scrapbooker should keep a bottle close at hand.

Bumps, Bleeds and Silhouettes— A Gallery of Crops

Three types of specialty crops give your pages more excitement:

Silhouette crop—You cut out all the background and leave only the subject. Use this when your background is distracting.

Bleed—Allows your image to extend off the edge of the paper. Your mind's eye fills in the details. Bleeds give a sense of drama and action.

Bump crop—Mentally draw a circle, oval, rectangle or square around your image. What extends beyond the perimeter of those shapes? That extended area is the bump. Bumping a part of the image out of the border adds interest.

TOOLBOX

SUPPLIES USED

Marker:
Fibracolor

Pen:
Micron by Sakura

Font:
CK Classic

Other Supplies:
Oval Cropper™ by
Shaping Memories

? STORY STARTERS

Our lives overlap with others in many venues: work, school, family, religion, hobbies, pet ownership and exercise. Use your scrapbook as a way to honor all the people who add joy to your life.

Pat's Birthday

She's not the secretary. She's not the administrative assistant. She's our QUEEN. Good Queen Pat. What would we do without her? She handles phone calls, customers, and so much more at David's business. When Susan called to remind me of Pat's birthday, we agreed that only the best was good enough for our Pat. So we had a long, lovely lunch at the Ritz. (December 1999)

TECHNIQUE: *Creating a Headline on Your Computer*

◄ Select a font (type style) and size on your computer. Print out the lettering. Color in the lettering with a marker. With a JG pen, draw a scalloped border around the lettering. Re-copy the border with a marker.

Add the features to a snowman. Use his scarf for a pattern and cut another scarf out of paper that compliments your page. Cut out two journaling boxes, one 2" x 5" and one 2" x 4". Crop one photo into an oval shape. ►

Customize Your Die Cuts

This cute snowman came with a ready made hat and scarf that I didn't use. For a quick pattern, trace around die cut pieces. With a plaid like this, you'll have to trace on the wrong side of the plaid paper to get your lines to show up.

Or, you can run a couple of lines of HERMAfix on the back, adhere the die cut piece to the desired paper, and trim around it.

◄ Cut out a round scalloped border with scissors. Mat it with solid paper that is cut with scallops. Mat all the other elements on an 8 ½" x 11" piece of paper. Affix the 8 ½" x 11" piece of paper to 12" x 12" background paper.

Mix and Match

Using an entire sheet of 8 ½" x 11" paper as a mat works well on a 12" x 12" background. You'll find more examples of mixing and matching paper sizes on pages 54, 56, 60 and 64.

Getting a Head (line) with Your Computer

One of the fastest and most flexible ways to create a headline or page title is on your computer.

1. Print out a sample of all your fonts so you can easily refer to them.

2. If the font is solid, you can either print it out in color or trace around it and color it in another color.

3. Invest in a lettering CD. The ones by Creating Keepsakes offer many lettering styles you'll use again and again.

4. For an effective headline that goes across your page, print out your headline in 42 point type or larger. Smaller type won't have enough impact.

TOOLBOX

SUPPLIES USED

Paper:
Keeping Memories
Alive

Pen:
Avery

Punch:
Leaf punches by
Emagination Crafts

Other Supplies:
Post-it Notes by 3M

? STORY STARTERS

You don't have to pur-
chase seasonal flowers
to enjoy them. Stop the
car, get out and be a
part of the world
around you.

Autumn's Face

No spring, nor summer
Beauty hath such grace,
As I have seen in
One autumnal face.
   —John Donne

We stopped at the greenhouse on the road to St. Albans to buy
mums. Then we discovered they were closed for the day.
(Fall 1999)

TECHNIQUE: *Adding an "Applique Pattern"*

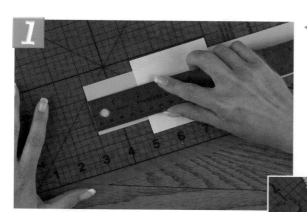

◄ Cut a strip of orange paper 2" x 10". At 2" intervals, cut it into squares. Punch leaves or use leaf die cuts to decorate the squares. From two pieces of 12" x 12" paper, cut one rectangle 9 ¼" x 10 ½" and one rectangle 10 ¼" x 10 ¾".

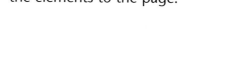

"Stitch" around the outside of the leaves and "hemstitch" around the outside of the 2" x 2" boxes. Mat the 9 ¼" x 10 ½" rectangle onto the 10 ¼" x 10 ¾" rectangle. Mat rectangles onto 12" x 12" background paper. ►

◄ "Hemstitch" around the smaller rectangle. Mat a 2" x 3 ½" journaling box. Journal in the box. I also journaled on the on the 9 ¼" x 10 ½" rectangle. Affix all the elements to the page.

Cardstock— What is It?

To the rest of the world, cardstock is an extra-thick heavy weight paper. To scrapbookers, cardstock means a solid paper, usually a tad heavier than the usual scrapbook paper.

Cardstock weight paper is your best bet for page backgrounds. You can affix multiple layers to it, and it won't sag or tear.

KMA (Keeping Memories Alive) has a splendid line of patterned papers that are heavy enough to support any embellishments.

If you do add elements to a lightweight background paper, you may wish to adhere that background paper to a piece of heavier stock.

Where the Ideas Come From...

A package of napkins I purchased in the grocery store had leaves on them with this kind of "stitching" on each block of color. One napkin made its way into my idea notebook. I randomly glue or tape pictures that appeal to me in the notebook and use it as a repository for idea starters.

A few places to look for graphic inspiration include:

- advertisements
- greeting cards
- clothes
- brochures
- catalogs
- paper goods (like napkins)
- magazines
- direct mail

SUPPLIES USED

Paper:
Page Topper™ by
Cock-A-Doodle Design

Chalk:
Decorating Chalks by
Craft-T Products

Stamp:
Stamps for Journaling
by Scrapbookin'
Stamps

Ink:
Stampin' Up

The best laid plans often go awry. What did you plan and what really happened?

Putt, Putt and Away—A Quick Round of Golf

Sure looks like Michael and Pasquales (David's Aunt Phyllis's grandson) are having fun. However, shortly after this photo Michael suddenly felt sick. Then the guys decided it was too hot to play golf, so they put away the clubs and ate ice cream instead. Actually, it was a smart move. The temperature continued to climb, and a heat advisory was announced. (August 2000)

TECHNIQUE: *Stamping a Journaling Box*

◀ Add chalk to your page title with a sponge brush. Leave the golf balls white.

Press your stamp onto the ink pad several times. Stamp the image on waste paper. Now stamp it on archival paper. Journal in the box. Cut out the journaling box and mat it. ▶

◀ Mat all the photos. Affix all the elements to the page, letting the bottom photo overlap the upper photos.

Scrapbookin' Stamps

Ever meet someone new and just click? I felt that way when I met Karen Greenstreet at a scrapbook show. Karen and her partner, Paige Harvey, have developed an entire line of stamps that help you journal.

For starters, your shopping list should include the square stamp shown here, the 5" x 1 $1/2$" straight lines stamp, the 3" x 3" straight lines stamp, and the oval thought bubble or oval speech bubble. After that, the sky's the limit since you can choose from flowerpots, cameras, newspapers, school paper, snowmen, balloons, and signs just to name a few.

Quick and Easy Stamping Techniques

Yes, stamping can be quick and easy! Here are a few tips:

1. Buy a black archival ink pad larger than your largest stamp. A small pad means taking a gob of time to ink your die (rubber face).

2. Buy a stamp cleaning tray, such as those sold by Stampin' Up. They really make clean up fast and easy.

3. Break your stamps in. Stamps seem to stamp best after they've been inked and stamped four or five times. Do this on waste paper, of course.

4. Stamp extras of images you use often. Extra journaling boxes are a great idea.

TOOLBOX

SUPPLIES USED

Paper:
Keeping Memories
Alive

Adhesive:
HERMAfix

Pens:
Zig
Micron by Sakura

Stickers:
Alphabet stickers by
Fresh & Funky®, by
One Heart… One Mind

Chalk:
Decorating Chalks by
Craft-T Products

Colored pencils:
Berol

? STORY STARTERS

Catch your pets following their instincts. What happened and how did you respond?

Lilly and the Lizard

*T*he cousins worked as a team to help Michael catch lizards in Florida during Christmas break 1999. One cousin was the spotter, one was the distractor, and Mike was the grabber. Here, Lexie and Michael search the woodpile for prey. The cousins kept their lizards in a plastic jar with holes in the lid. Once lizards were in the jar, we had to watch out for Lilly, the cat. She would spot the lizard through the plastic walls and try to swat at it. Finally, we put the jar up high on the mantelpiece.

TECHNIQUE: *Using Colored Pencils*

◀ Color in your letter stickers with a marker. Remove the letters and adhere them to the page. Mat your photos as desired.

Photocopy and enlarge the page or ▶ use the template from www.scrapbookstorytelling.com as a pattern. If the template is used as a pattern, affix it with HERMAfix. Trace it on charcoal paper and cut it out.

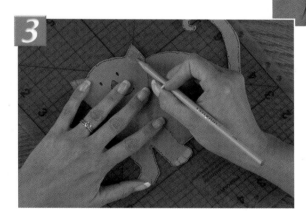

◀ Draw features with a Micron or other fine-tipped pen. Outline the cat with a Micron pen in a wiggly line. Color in the cat markings with pencils. Affix all elements to the page.

Colored Pencil Coloring Techniques

1. Start with your lightest color and then add darker colors progressively. If you start dark, you can erase. If you start light, you can add and shade.

2. For the most natural look, blend two or more colors together.

3. For a dark, solid color, crosshatch your pencil marks. Make strokes from the lower left to the upper right, then go from the lower right to the upper left.

4. Color areas with a depression darker and areas where there is a high spot lighter. (It's called *shading*, and it takes practice to get it right.)

5. Use a good eraser. You can totally erase your coloring or, by lightly stroking what you've colored, you can soften the color.

Buy Quality Pencils for Best Results

The colored pencils you buy in toy stores are bound to disappoint you. Artist quality pencils lay down a layer of color with very little pressure. Poor quality pencils are more likely to tear a hole in your paper.

With good quality pencils, you can blend colors easily. Furthermore, the good ones come in a vast array of colors which are sold individually so that when one color is down to a nub you don't have to buy another entire set.

Best way to buy good quality colored pencils? Look for a sale or a coupon for use at your local art or craft supply store.

These are one of the few products where price really indicates quality.

SUPPLIES USED

Paper:
Keeping Memories
Alive

Stickers:
Water sticker strip by
Frances Meyer, Inc.

Country Garden Border
Set by Annette Allen
Watkin, ©1999
Printworks

Lettering:
Alphabet stickers,
©1996 Design Originals
by Suzanne McNeill

? STORY STARTERS

*Take time to observe
nature. The courtship
of these swans unfold-
ed before our eyes.
What is happening in
your back yard?*

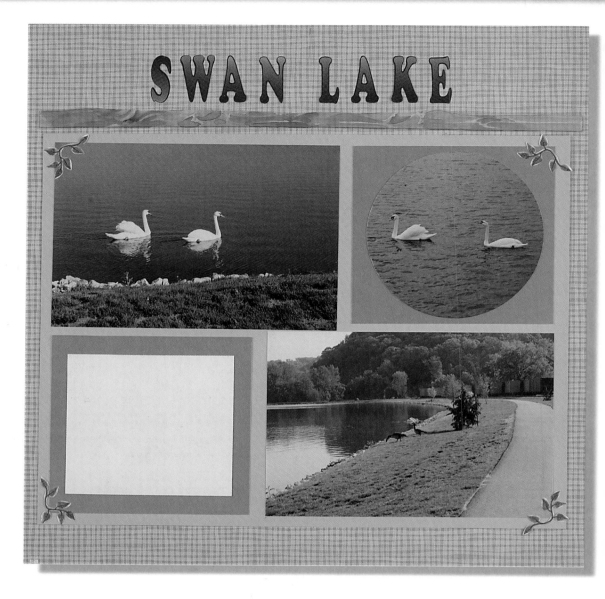

Swan Lake: The Triumph of the Swan

One mild spring day in 2000, a lone swan appeared at the lake at St. Albans. Michael pointed it out on the way home from school. The solo swan lingered for weeks. Since swans mate for life, Michael and I wondered what happened to its mate. "Maybe," he said, "This swan went on ahead of his wife to find a good home." He must have been right because about a month after the first swan came, the second appeared.

TECHNIQUE: *Embossing a Stamped Image*

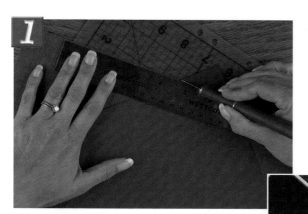

◀ Tilt the solid paper and adhere it to the patterned background. Trim off any edges that overhang. Cut a journaling box 2" x 4". Draw scallops around the perimeter with a JG pen. Go over the scallop border with a metallic pen.

Stamp letters to create a headline. Trace around the letters with JG pen and draw a scalloped border. Trace over the JG pen border with a metallic gold pen. Trim around the letters. ▶

◀ Cut a rectangle 3 1/2" x 4 3/4". Ink a corner stamp with gold pigment ink. Stamp the image. Emboss it with gold embossing powder. Add to each corner of the rectangular mat. Oval crop one photo. Create an oval border of solid paper to mat the oval photo. Affix the photo and the oval mat to the rectangle.

Go for the Gold

It's amazing how the merest hint of precious metals adds richness to your pages. A few ways to go for the gold:

- gold ink
- metallic embellishments
- embossing powder
- gold foil (this is applied with a special adhesive you can buy in stamping stores)
- metallic paper

Adding a New Dimension with Embossing

Stamp with a slow-drying pigment ink, and you can add dimension to your image with embossing. It's super for adding a bit of spunk. In particular, you need to emboss over metallic inks to safeguard your photos. The steps are simple:

1. Always use a pigment ink for its slow-drying properties.
2. Pour embossing powder onto an inked image.
3. Tap off the extra powder. Use a small bristle brush (paintbrush) to brush off any excess powder that isn't part of the image.
4. Hold the stamped image over a light bulb so the the paper is heated up. Or direct hot air onto the image with an embossing gun.
5. Heat it until the powder rises.

Be careful with your heat source, or you'll scorch your paper.

SUPPLIES USED

Paper:
Flags by Frances Meyer

Stickers:
Letter stickers by
Paper Adventures

Mrs. Grossman's
Design Lines

Marker:
Zig

Pen:
Avery

? STORY STARTERS

Share your unique family preferences. Because my husband sells pianos, we are often surrounded with superb musicians. Photos of our friends singing is uniquely "Slan." What's your family's forte?

July 4th, 1993

Our first 4th of July in our new house in St. Louis, we invited all the folks from David's store to come and celebrate. Clockwise: Daryl and Mona, our son Michael, and Mick and Ken. With so many fine musicians, we naturally gathered around the piano. Soon we were all singing patriotic songs. The children were surprised to hear how many songs we all knew. I hadn't heard "The Battle Hymn of the Republic" for years, and I had forgotten how stirring the song is.

TECHNIQUE: *Creating Tile Lettering with Stickers*

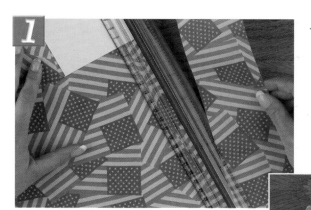

◀ Cut a strip of patterned paper 2 1/4" x 12". Cut a strip of white paper 1" x 11". Affix the patterned paper strip to the left hand margin of your page. Create a journaling box 2" x 3 3/4". Mat the journaling box. Journal in the box. Crop and mat the photos.

Measure and mark 1" intervals on your white strip of paper with the JG pen. Using a marker, go back over the lines, making a wide band of color. Using a marker, draw a border on the top and bottom of the strip. ▶

◀ Center the letter stickers inside each box. Run a stripe of HERMAfix along the back of the white strip. Cut apart the boxes by slicing through the lines between each. Affix all the elements to the page, spacing letter tiles evenly along the patterned stripe. Add a Design Line to the edge of the patterned paper.

Tip!

Head for the Border on Your 12" x 12" Page

Since the 12" x 12" size is symmetrical, the temptation is great to line up your elements evenly. If you do, you could wind up with a totally boring page. By adding a border strip to one of the sides, your working space has an interesting off-center focus.

Tip!

Pattern or Solid? How to Decide

Of course, on this page, the border could have been a solid and the background could have been flags. In general, though, the busier your photos are the simpler your background should be OR the wider your mats should be. To get four pictures and a journaling box on the right, thin mats were a must.

Tackling the Tedium of Tiles

Tile lettering gives a neat, finished look to your page. With the tile style, you can add an extra touch of color or pattern behind your letters. Say that you want to use yellow lettering. You can't use it on other light colors or it will disappear. But, backing the yellow with a colored tile solves your design problem.

Unfortunately, tiles can be time consuming, especially if you cut the tiles in advance. The reason? Small squares of paper are much harder to handle than one bigger strip. By coloring the edges between the strips in advance, you also make the size of the paper work for you. Cut the strip longer than you need, so you have extra tiles in case you have trouble getting your marker edging just right.

SUPPLIES USED

Paper:
Gingham paper by
Paper Adventures

Stickers:
Letter stickers by
Paper Adventures

Flower stickers by
Mrs. Grossman

Pens:
Avery

Other Supplies:
The Journaling Genie
Vanishing Ink Pen

? STORY STARTERS

Think of your dearest friends. What are the qualities that make them so attractive to you? Find a way to illustrate those qualities.

Elaine Floyd cradling Eliza Paige -- Spring 2000, Chesterfield, Missouri.

Elaine Floyd Holding Eliza—Spring 2000, Chesterfield MO

Sometimes one photo is a story in and of itself. See how sweetly Elaine is cradling Eliza—even though Eliza is not her child. This image has captured an important aspect of my best friend's personality.

TECHNIQUE: *Enhancing Page Design with Matted Tiles*

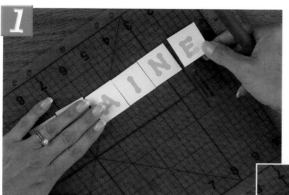

◀ Cut a strip of paper 1 ¼" wide and approximately 8" long. Use a JG pen to mark the paper at 1 ¼" intervals. Lay down the letter stickers on the paper strip. Apply a stripe of HERMAfix to the back of the lettering tiles. Cut the strip into squares at intervals.

Affix the lettering tiles to a strip of gingham 1 ³/4" wide and at least 9" long (or two shorter strips). Use the squares of gingham to help you center the tiles. Cut the tiles apart at intervals. ▶

◀ Cut out the center frame on 8 ½" x 11" paper. Back the opening with gingham. Crop the photo to fit. Adhere the photo to the page. Affix all the elements to a 12" x 12" page. Use red pen to add color to the center of the flowers. Add the flower sticker to the mat around the letters.

Gung Ho for Gingham

Gingham, checks, plaids and stripes offer short cuts for a busy scrapper. These patterns are typically arranged at regular intervals, so you can use the pattern to help you accurately space page elements.

Organizing Your Paper

To make it faster to find the paper I want, I've organized my paper with Post-it Note labels. On each label is a category: Plaids, Stripes, Gingham, Children, Babies, Celebrations, Holidays, Pets, Outdoors, Travel, Plants, Flowers, Weather, and Landscapes. The paper is in a file cabinet with the notes sticking up like file tabs. Solid papers are in a separate file by color families.

The 12"x 12" papers are in an open milk crate file. Having some semblance of order really saves time.

Customizing Your Patterned Papers

Perhaps you've had a similar experience: You have an appealing piece of paper with a pattern, but the color isn't quite right or the picture doesn't exactly match another page element. Don't give up! Instead, grab your colored pencils or markers.

Unless the paper is coated, you can lay down a layer of color over the existing image. So the daisies on the facing page could have been colored peach and with the addition of yellow, the roses and fan could have been a deep shade of orange. Instead, I added red marker to the center of some of the purple flowers so they'd match the red in the flower sticker on the mat of the final E.

My point? Even with a printed image, it's still PAPER. Use your patterned paper as a point of departure for your creativity.

? STORY STARTERS

Capture a child's passion. My son loves hunting for critters. What is it your kid could do 24-hours a day? Write about it.

SUPPLIES USED

Paper:	Plaid paper by Paper Pizazz
Stamps:	Stamps for Journaling by Scrapbookin' Stamps
Ink:	Dauber Duos by Tsukineko
Pen:	Fibracolor
Lettering:	Déja Views Designer Letters
Stickers:	Frog stickers by HMK, CDS
Other Supplies:	Circle cutter by Fiskars

Good Frog Hunting

On a bright Spring morning in 2000, Michael, Kevin (our Bichon Frise) and I went to Queeny Park for an "explore." As usual Michael caught dozens of tiny frogs. You can even see the head of one little guy between Mike's grubby fingers. The slow moving creeks were perfect for ambushing amphibians. I tried to keep Kevin out of the water, but he wound up soaked and muddy. Despite the mess, the blooming trees and spring flowers made for an idyllic day.

TECHNIQUE: *Working on a 12" x 12" Double Spread*

◀ Cut a strip of paper 4 ³/4" x 12". Tape both sheets of the 12" x 12" paper together on the back. Circle crop two photos. Mat the photos with larger circles of white paper. Mat one on a square of red-orange paper. Mat all the photos.

Using the 3" x 3" journaling line stamp, stamp lines on white paper. Next, stamp the 5" x 1 ¹/2" journaling lines onto white paper. Mat both with gingham. Cut a 1" x 15" strip of white paper. Use a marker to frame the boxes as on page 60. Add the letter stickers to the inside of the boxes. ▶

◀ Run a strip of HERMAfix on the back of the white lettering tiles. Cut apart the lettering tiles. Affix all elements except the frog stickers to the page. Lift the journaling tiles and slip the frog stickers beneath. Affix the stickers to the page and cut apart the pages.

Creating Visual Unity for Spreads

When creating a double page spread, you will want the two pages to appear as one unit. You can use two sheets of the same paper or...

1. Run a strip of paper across both pages. The paper can go across the tops, the bottoms, the middle or on a diagonal. The resulting horizon of color or pattern will guide the eyes.

2. Use a border around the outside perimeter of the two pages. Do not run the border up the center between the pages. The border acts as a visual fence holding all the elements inside.

3. Create mirroring or matching patterns on the facing pages.

4. Run the page title across the two pages. Make sure your wording reads from left to right.

Better Photos— Step In and Step Away

After you snap a photo, try this technique to add a different vantage point: Step away from your subject by 10 paces. Take the photo. Go back to your original position. Now step in toward your subject by 10 paces.

Notice the close up of the little frog in my son's hands. This photo adds tremendous interest to the pages. First, it makes clear what Michael was doing. Second, because the focus is tight, it breaks up the uniformity of the other shots, which were all taken at approximately the same distance. And third, it emphasizes the little boy feel of the activity and the page.

Routine is the enemy of the creative. Make it a point to try something new with each page.

TOOLBOX

SUPPLIES USED

Paper:
Frances Meyer

Lettering:
Dot Tip Alphabet by
Fresh & Funky from
One Heart… One Mind

Markers:
Zig and Marvy

? STORY STARTERS

*Have you put a lot of
energy into a project?
What was it? How did
it turn out?*

How Does My Garden Grow?

This year was the summer of the garden. I filled pots with petunias and geraniums for the front of the house. I transplanted flowers from Grandma Marge's house. The four o' clocks beside the house (upper photo) weathered the trip from Vincennes well and struggled for a few weeks during blistering temperatures. Then, suddenly they took off! In fact, David keeps threatening to cut the plants back.

TECHNIQUE: *Working with Pre-Printed Frames*

◀ Trim out the inside of the frames with a craft knife. Use the middle box to trace a pattern onto white archival paper. Journal on the archival paper and center it under the frame. Affix the journaling box with photo safe tape from behind. Trim the excess paper.

Color in large and small letter stickers with markers. Cut a strip of white paper 1" x 3". Affix large letter stickers to the strip. Use Post-it Notes to temporarily mark a 3 1/4" border down the left side of your paper. Center small letter stickers inside the border. ▶

◀ Trim about 1/4" off the top, bottom and sides of the frame paper. Run strips of HERMAfix across the back of the paper with frames on it. Adhere the paper to the page, leaving a small outside border of solid paper around the frame paper. Slip photos under the openings. Affix the photos and trim them.

Tip!

Make Your Mark with Uncolored Letter Stickers

Still have that shopping list? Add Alphabet Stickers by Fresh & Funky to it. The letters come in a variety of styles—see pages 42 and 52—and sizes. If you buy different sizes, buy stickers from the same type style family. That way you can create a headline in two differing sizes, as you see here.

Because the paper for these stickers is slick, you'll want to give your ink a few moments to dry before trying to lift the stickers from the page.

You'll love how smoothly Zig markers lay down color on these stickers.

What Comes First? The Paper or the Idea?

Doesn't matter! Sometimes a cool piece of paper will generate a great page idea. Sometimes a great page idea will have to wait for the right paper. One way to keep the ideas flowing is to create your own idea file or idea notebook.

1. Designate a spiral bound notebook or a ring-binder with paper for your ideas.

2. Categorize ideas: Layout, Backgrounds, Themes, Lettering, Journaling.

3. Write, sketch or tape in ideas you come across for each theme.

Seem like a lot of time and effort? The payoff is huge. Becky Higgins, staff member of *Creating Keepsakes* scrapbook magazine, relies heavily on her idea notebook for inspiration. You will, too.

?STORY STARTERS

Record a child's play life. Here my niece shows her love of costume. How do your children play? What props do they choose? How did it turn out?

Dress for Success

Let's see—a chef, a mermaid and a bride. Who's behind all these costumes? Rachel, of course! Obviously, the child does NOT lack imagination. After seeing her Uncle Kevin's wedding, being a bride was her top priority. Her mother, my sister, Margaret made the lovely train by tying on a tablecloth. Wasn't that clever? (Fall 1999)

TECHNIQUE: *Using Clear Stamps*

◀ With a JG pen, outline a page title box 3 ¹/₄" x 6." Stamp your headline on white archival paper centering it within the box. Cut out the box. Cut a journaling box 1 ¹/₂" x 3". Write your journaling.

Ink a clear corner stamp. Stamp the image in the corner, slightly turning the stamp each time so that the stamped image opens out onto the page. Use a marker to add a red dot to the center of the corner stamp image. ▶

◀ Oval crop the photos. Bump crop one photo if desired. Run a line of HERMAfix on the back of all the elements. Affix all the elements to the page.

A Clearly Better Approach to Stamping

See-through stamps take the hassle out of stamping. Since you can see right through the die (the image) and the handle, stamp placement is a breeze. These tips will get you stamping up a storm:

1. Immediately ink all your clear stamps with black archival ink. Clean off any excess ink. The ink will stain the die so you can easily identify your stamps. (See the stamp in #2 for an example.)

2. Practice using your stamps, particularly those with an interchangeable handle. (I'm such a bozo. I didn't realize there was a handle in the kit and tried to stamp just using the die. I got ink all over me.)

3. Adjust the pressure you use to stamp an image. Clear stamps are "squishier." Too much pressure will distort the stamped image.

Crop Etiquette: What to Know Before You Go

I was as lost as an Easter egg when I attended my first crop. A crop is a marathon scrapbooking session. Usually these are held in stores or during conventions or by Creative Memories consultants.

Here are a few questions you might ask before you attend the crop:

• Is there a charge?

• How do they handle no-shows? (Some charge you but give you a credit to attend another crop.)

• What materials will be available for use?

• What materials will be available for purchase?

• What's the coin of the realm? Cash, checks or credit cards?

• Will there be any sort of demonstration?

• What should you bring?

TOOLBOX

SUPPLIES USED

Paper:
Keeping Memories
Alive

Page Topper™ by
Cock-A-Doodle Design

STORY STARTERS

It's normal for a child to have trepidation about a new experience. Document how it came out. Was his/her fear justified?

Camping

Michael wasn't sure how he'd like Camp Wyman. The grin on his face when I picked him up says it all. Camp was AWESOME. The camp was scheduled for early in the school year to allow the students and teachers to come together as a team. Michael particularly enjoyed getting to know Mr. B, his science and math teacher. This was Mr. B's first year as a full-time teacher, after shifting from a career in another field. Our verdict? Mr. B was meant to teach. 'Cause Mr. B is AWESOME! (Fall 1999)

TECHNIQUE: *Tearing Paper for Special Effects*

◄ Tear pieces of 12" x 12" paper into "mound" shapes. Lay these shapes on the bottom of your page to create a landscape. Crop the photos as desired. Cut a 4 1/4" x 4 1/4" journaling box.

Affix a silhouette cropped photo to a 3" x 5 1/2" mat. Mat the pre-printed page title. ►

The Joy of Disposable Cameras

Don't get me wrong. For the most part, the better the camera, the better your photos will be. But, I still love disposables once in a while.

For this page, I sent along a disposable camera with my son to camp. The picture of Mr. B is the ONLY useable photo that he brought back. As a bonus, Michael managed to get the bunk beds and the interior of the cabin in the background.

I supplemented his photo with two of mine: 1) the look on Michael's face when he said, "Awesome" and 2) the pile of clothes and equipment that came back after camp.

When you hand a child a disposable camera, you'll see the world from a kid's viewpoint. That's reason enough to love these inexpensive tools.

◄ Arrange all of the page elements and adhere them on the page. Slide the trunks of the trees down into the torn pieces of paper at the page bottom. Overlap the tree branches on the page and on the other trees.

How to Rip Your Paper Into Shape

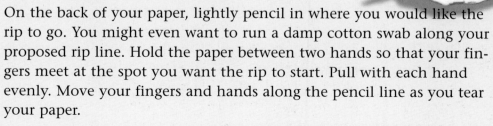

On the back of your paper, lightly pencil in where you would like the rip to go. You might even want to run a damp cotton swab along your proposed rip line. Hold the paper between two hands so that your fingers meet at the spot you want the rip to start. Pull with each hand evenly. Move your fingers and hands along the pencil line as you tear your paper.

For a different look, try ripping paper that is only top-coated with color instead of paper that is a solid color all the way through. Remember, too, as you tear the paper, it will have a right side and a wrong side. I like to use the side where the tear has varying heights.

? STORY STARTERS

Beyond our biological family is the extended family of friends we include in our hugs and prayers. Whose friendship has become an important part of your family's life? How do your individual family members interact with other families you enjoy?

Eliza

Nancy is my neighbor, my aerobics instructor and my friend. Our family followed her pregnancy with great excitement. We were delighted to hear that Eliza had joined Nancy and Mark's family. It's such fun to have a little girl nearby to dote on, since my nieces live so far away. Here Eliza makes one of her earliest social appearances where her sweet nature and winning smile captivated a room full of women.

TECHNIQUE: *Using Embossed Photo Mats*

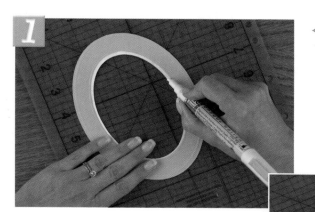

◀ Use an opaque white marker to outline the inner oval of the embossed oval paper frame.

Slide the photo under the frame. ▶ Center the photo and affix it to the frame. Cut off any of the photo that extends past the frame. Add a pre-printed embellishment to the lower left corner of the frame.

◀ Mat the photos. Affix all the elements to the page. Cut a 5 $\frac{1}{2}$" x 5 $\frac{1}{2}$" journaling box and mat it. Align the middle letter with the mid-point measurement of the journaling box (2 $\frac{3}{4}$") and lay down the letter. Lay down the rest of the letters, working from the center to the outside.

Quicker Pages with Papers and Supplies that Coordinate

When a manufacturer like Keeping Memories Alive (KMA) offers an entire line of papers and products, you can save time and money. No more trying to match up colors. No more trying to match up styles. That tedious work is done for you. For scrapbookers who aren't comfortable with their ability to mix and match products, coordinated paper and product lines are the way to go.

Coordinated lines might also be your best bet if your time and money are limited. You can't go wrong with an album of pages built entirely on one manufacturer's line. By sticking to one maker, you'll build in visual continuity from page to page. You factor out waste and aggravation. The result? A polished project.

Ever Wonder How Modern Scrapbooking Started?

In response to a church assignment on family history, Marielen Christensen began to research why photos faded. As she learned about the role of acid, Marielen searched for acid-free products she could use on her own scrapbook pages. As her personal stockpile of archival products grew, Marielen was swamped with requests from others who heard about her discoveries. It quickly became evident to her and her husband that they could expand their product line and their service to others.

Today Keeping Memories Alive is one of the most respected scrapbook sources in this field. If you're ever in Spanish Fork, Utah, visit their outlet and pay your respects to the First Lady of Scrapbooking.

TOOLBOX

SUPPLIES USED

Paper:
Dog Bones by
Design Originals

Red/Blue Grid by
Paperbilities III, © 1997
MPR Associates

Lettering:
Puffy Letters stencil by
Provo Craft

Pen:
Marvy LePlume II

? STORY STARTERS

I love it when other people play along! Obviously, the folks at this DQ understood pet owners. Who appreciates your pet and why?

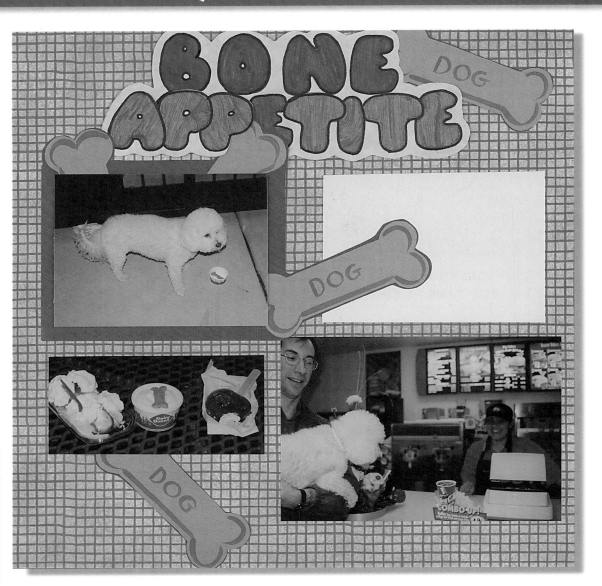

Bone Appetite

On our way back from visiting David's father in Bloomington, Illinois, we decided to make a quick stop at a Dairy Queen. Michael and David not only ordered ice cream for us humans, but they also brought back "doggy" ice cream for Kevin, who is always a big hit when he visits my father-in-law's retirement community. Imagine our delight at the dog biscuit in the ice cream cup! Later, David carried Kevin to the counter so he could thank the DQ workers in person—er, in dog.

TECHNIQUE: *Taking Embellishments from Patterned Paper*

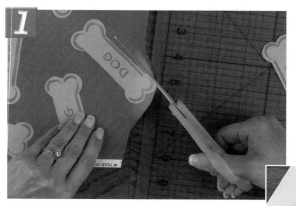

◄ Cut bones out of the patterned paper. You'll need at least five bones.

Use a letter template to lightly trace ► the lettering with colored pencils. Color in the letters with markers. Align the letter template over the colored letters and re-outline the letters in black with a marker. Cut out the headline, cutting into the bottom word between letters.

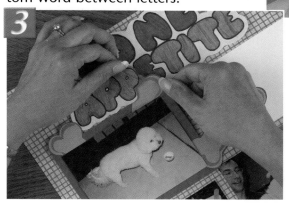

◄ Crop photos as desired. Mat one photo. Cut a 3 1/4" x 4 1/2" journaling box. Affix all the elements. Slide the bones onto the page and affix them as desired. Slide one bone into the cut between the letters of the second headline word.

How Odd... A Design Tip

Whenever you add embellishments, always use an odd number. When you add an even number, the eye tends to match up the elements. An odd number is more visually interesting.

Carry a Camera Everywhere

How many times have you said to yourself, "Gee, I wish I had my camera?" You never know when you'll have a great photo opportunity. Get in the habit of carrying your camera with you all the time. Unless I'm photographing a specific event, I keep my camera loaded with Kodak Max 400 ASA film. It's the most flexible for different conditions. Keeping a spare camera battery in your purse is not only a smart idea, but one that saves you a precious moment and money. (Ever buy a battery from a gift shop? YE-OWWW.)

Too Big, Too Bold and Totally Overwhelming?

See if you've had this experience: When you get together that nifty paper you bought and the photos you took, your pictures are totally lost in the shuffle. Groan. It happens. The paper seduced you, kiddo. Here's what to do next:

1. Cut the paper into strips and use it as stripes or a border.

2. Enlarge your primary photo on a Kodak Picture Maker machine. Use the large version of the picture on your page.

3. Give your photos a wide solid paper mat. Or double-mat your photos, first using solid paper and then using the patterned paper as a mat.

4. Cut the paper and use it as embellishments, as I did here.

SUPPLIES USED

Paper:
David Walker for
Frances Meyer

Ink:
Dauber Duos by
Tsukineko

Pen:
Avery

**STORY
STARTERS**

*Sharing the traditions
of another city or cul-
ture is always reward-
ing. What did your
family try in new sur-
roundings? What was
the outcome?*

Skating at Woolman Rink

While visiting New York City before Christmas, David and Michael decided to go ice skating at Woolman Rink in Central Park. The day was beautiful and the weather was so mild! Soon the boys joined the other skaters going 'round and 'round. I snapped all these photos from the same place at the rink side. The guys enjoyed ice skating so much that they woke up early the next morning and skated at Rockefeller Center. (December 1999)

TECHNIQUE: *Customizing Pre-Printed Paper*

◄ Create a blue mat 7" x 8 3/4". Use a JG pen to trace around the outside of the blue mat onto 12" x 12" paper. Use a craft knife to cut around the outside of the trees that will overlap the blue mat. Cut out the words "Tree Farm" from the sign, if desired.

Use a Dauber Duo pen to make white "snowflakes" on the blue background. Add a 5 1/4" x 7 1/2" white journaling box. ►

◄ Align photo horizons as explained on page 43. Crop photos as needed and tape them together on the back. Affix the photos to the bottom of the page. Replace "Tree Farm" with new signage by slipping the paper under the opening in the sign, writing in the letters, and affixing the new paper.

Snow Easy with Dauber Duos

Can you believe how easy it is to make soft snow flakes with this Dauber Duo? You can also use a Dauber Duo to ink a stamp or to create lettering with your letter stencil. Here's how:

1. Hold your letter template down firmly on the paper.

2. Cover unwanted letters with a Post-it Note.

3. Gently stipple the desired letter with the sponge.

4. Wait a minute and stipple the letter again, if you want more intense color.

5. Let the ink dry a moment and then lift the template straight up and off the paper. If you slide the template it may smear the ink.

6. Wipe the letter template clean and proceed to your next letter.

How Quick and How Easy Does Scrapbooking Need to Be?

We're all pressed for time. So how do we find time for scrapbooking?

Be organized. I've said it before, and I'll repeat it. Searching for supplies is a drain on your time and energy.

Work on several pages. Reach an impasse? Slip an unfinished page in an archival page protector and go on to another page. While you're working on one page, you'll figure out what to do with the first one.

Make scrapbook products work overtime. Learn all the ways you can use your products. For example, you can use HERMAfix to permanently affix elements or to hold them temporarily while you make decisions.

Take in a lot of ideas. Subscribe to scrapbooking magazines to keep up with the latest and greatest products and technique tips.

Index

Glossary of Terms

Acid—a chemical on our skin and in photos that will, over time, destroy a photographic image.

Archival—that which will not self-destruct or destroy other items over time.

Background paper—the paper on which your page elements are mounted.

Bleed—extending an image off the edges of the paper.

Bump crop—cutting a photo so that one area extends outside the border or into the mat.

Cardstock—solid color archival paper of a heavy weight.

CK OK—an approval process conducted by Creating Keepsakes magazine to assure scrapbookers of archivally safe products.

Chalk—a colored calcium carbonate substance used to mark on paper.

Circle cropper—a tool designed to cut a smooth circle in a variety of sizes.

Craft knife—a tool with a replaceable blade for cutting.

Craft mat—a protective surface for use while working on crafts.

Crop—a get together for the purpose of scrapbooking pages.

Cropping—cutting a photo.

Deckle scissors—decorative scissors with an irregular blade.

Decorative scissors—scissors with blades that create a pattern in the paper they cut.

Design Line (by Mrs. Grossman) — a brand name sticker tape that comes in colors.

Design transfer—the process of copying an image.

Die cut—a solid color or printed paper image punched out by a metal die.

Disposable camera—a camera designed to be used only one time.

Double page spread—two facing scrapbook pages.

Elements—page pieces.

Embellishment—a page element added for decorative purposes.

Font—as used in scrapbooking, a type style.

Headlines—see *page titles*

HERMAfix—a brand name adhesive that rolls on in small dots, is repositionable, and is easily removed.

Journaling—writing or telling your story with words.

Journaling boxes—areas where writing will go.

The Journaling Genie Vanishing Ink Pen—a brand name of a pen by Chatterbox with a photo-safe ink that disappears over a period of 24 hours.

Laminate—to seal within thin layers.

Layout—the design of elements on a scrapbook page.

Letter stickers—stickers created in the shape of the alphabet.

NOTES:

Scrapbooking has borrowed terms from other disciplines and assigned its own set of definitions. I've tried to share these "stolen" terms to help you avoid confusion.

Light box—a clear surface with a light underneath used for copying materials.

Matting—backing a photo or page element with a second piece of paper.

Micron pen—a brand name fine tipped archival marker by Sakura.

Oval cropper—a tool designed to cut a smooth oval in a variety of sizes.

Overhead transparency—a clear, plastic sheet on which an image can be printed, and which is usually used with an overhead projector.

Page title (page topper or headline)—the dominant words on a page that introduce your topic.

Page protector—an archivally safe plastic sleeve you slip over your scrapbook page.

Panorama page protector—a protective sleeve designed to display two pages side by side.

Paper piecing—creating an image by using pieces of paper.

Paper trimmer or **personal trimmer**—a device with a blade and a surface used for cutting paper.

Pattern— a design to be used to create a page element.

Patterned paper—paper pre-printed with a design.

Photo safe—material that will not destroy photographic images.

Photo splits (double-sided tape squares or photo stickers)—double-sided squares of tape for securing page elements.

Point—a unit of measure for type, 72 points equal one inch.

Pop-it Up Dot—brand name by Cut-It-Up for a round piece of adhesive with a foam center to lift your elements up off the page.

Post-it Note—a brand name repositionable paper product by 3M.

Punch—a hand held tool using a metal die to cut shapes.

Silhouette crop—cutting away the background from a photo.

SoFJ—Site of Future Journaling or a blank space where your writing will go.

Stickers—printed images with an adhesive backing.

Story Starters—ideas to help you save your family stories and memories.

Template—a cut pattern to be used as a guide. In scrapbooking, a template and a stencil are used interchangeably as terms, although a stencil is usually of lighter weight material than a template.

Tracing paper (tissue paper)—see-through paper used to copy a design.

un-du—a brand name archivally safe liquid designed to unstick adhesives without ruining your page or paper.

Vellum—a high quality transparent paper.

Other Titles for Scrapbookers and Storytellers...

ISBN: 1-930500-01-7
80 pages (2001); $14.99

Storytelling with Rubber Stamps

Create pages that better tell your stories by using rubber stamps to make your own borders, backgrounds, embellishments, page toppers, frames and more.

You can scrapbook subjects most crafters can't because stamps give you the ability to create the supporting elements you need. You'll also learn frugal tips for affordable stamping—you'll even see how to use common household items like a pencil eraser as a stamp.

Coming Spring 2001:

ISBN: 1-930500-03-3
80 pages (2001); $14.99

One Minute Journaling shows how to capture your stores as they're happening using one-minute journaling methods. Then, you'll see how to get your stories onto your pages in under a minute!

ISBN: 0-9630222-8-8
128 pages (1999); $19.99

Scrapbook Storytelling

Save family stories and memories with photos, journaling and your own creativity

See how to document stories—from a quick sentence to page after scrapbook page. The book is full of ways to recover stories from the past, discover the stories in the present and create stories that light the path to the future.

With easily understood steps for documenting stories, readers then choose to combine narrative with photos, journals, memorabilia and more.

ISBN: 0-9630222-7-X
128 pages (1998); $19.99

Creating Family Newsletters

123 ideas for sharing memorable moments with family and friends

Creating Family Newsletters contains ideas and inspiration that makes a newsletter "doable" by anyone, regardless of age or writing and design ability. Through over 123 color examples, you'll see which type of newsletter is for you—text-only, poems, photo scrapbooks, cards, letters, genealogy, e-mail or Web sites.

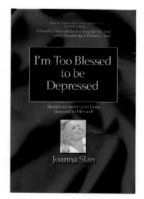

ISBN: 1-930500-04-1
208 pages (2001); $14.99

I'm Too Blessed to be Depressed is filled with inspirational stories and guided journaling that provide the perfect prescription for the blues.

? STORY STARTERS

If you've enjoyed the Story Starters throughout this book, be sure to sign up at www.scrapbookstorytelling.com for my free monthly broadcast of more ideas. Click the Free Newsletter button on the home page.

File Edit View Go Bookmarks Communicator Help

Netscape: Scrapbook Storytelling

Back Forward Reload Home Search Netscape Images Print Security Shop Stop

Location: http://www.scrapbookstorytelling.com/

Tips
Page Ideas
New Products
Events
Templates
Suppliers
Contact Us

Scrapbook Storytelling

Your link to saving everyday stories
with Joanna Campbell Slan

Scrapping Snippets

What's New?

Its All Greek to Me ... Here's the Greeking that Joanna Slan mentioned in this month's issue of Creating Keepsakes. Copy and paste it into a word processing file. Consider naming the file "Greeking" so you can easily find it when you need it to hold a journaling space for your scrapbook pages.

Question of the Month ... How do you handle awkward stories in your scrapbook?

There are often stories we want to save for future generations but may not want them on our coffee table. Joanna shares some ideas.

Attention Scrapbook Store Owners ... If you are interested in carrying Joanna's books in your store, please e-mail us at savetales@aol.com so we can provide you with wholesale information and other special goodies to help you and your customers save stories.

Are you ready for more ideas on storytelling... Joanna is working fast and furiously this summer on two new books for scrapbookers, Storytelling with Rubber Stamps and Quick & Easy Pages. Reserve your copies today.

Free Newsletter

Sign up to receive monthly Story Starters from Joanna Slan and news as the site is updated.

This is NOT the end. It's just the beginning!

Let's keep in touch—Visit my Web site at
http://www.scrapbookstorytelling.com

There, you'll find the templates mentioned in this book, new page ideas, tips and more! Plus, you'll be the first to know about my new products, free templates, and free monthly Story Starters by e-mail.

The story continues... and you can be a part of it.